Lecture Notes in Computer Science 8990

Commenced Publication in 1973
Founding and Former Series Editors:
Gerhard Goos, Juris Hartmanis, and Jan van Leeuwen

More information about this series at http://www.springer.com/series/8637

Abdelkader Hameurlain · Josef Küng
Roland Wagner · Devis Bianchini
Valeria De Antonellis · Roberto De Virgilio (Eds.)

Transactions on Large-Scale Data- and Knowledge-Centered Systems XIX

Special Issue on Big Data and Open Data

 Springer

Editors-in-Chief

Abdelkader Hameurlain
IRIT, Paul Sabatier University
Toulouse
France

Roland Wagner
FAW, University of Linz
Linz
Austria

Josef Küng
FAW, University of Linz
Linz
Austria

Guest Editors

Devis Bianchini
University of Brescia
Brescia
Italy

Roberto De Virgilio
University of Rome III
Rome
Italy

Valeria De Antonellis
University of Brescia
Brescia
Italy

ISSN 0302-9743   ISSN 1611-3349   (electronic)
Lecture Notes in Computer Science
ISBN 978-3-662-46561-5   ISBN 978-3-662-46562-2   (eBook)
DOI 10.1007/978-3-662-46562-2

Library of Congress Control Number: 2015932976

Springer Heidelberg New York Dordrecht London

Printed on acid-free paper

Springer-Verlag GmbH Berlin Heidelberg is part of Springer Science+Business Media
(www.springer.com)

LNCS Transactions on Large-Scale Data- and Knowledge-Centered Systems (TLDKS)

Special Issue on Big Data and Linked Open Data

Linked Data and Big Data have been featured in recent years due to growing interest. Proper use of enabling technologies meant for these two kinds of data is a critical success factor in the evolution of the Web. The Linked Data perspective inspired research efforts for building, maintaining, and exploiting the Web as a global database, where resources are identified (by means of URIs), semantically described (by means of RDF), and connected through RDF links. This perspective goes beyond the potential of Web 2.0, enabling people and applications to discover new linked information in an unexpected way, according to an explorative perspective. Big Data emphasizes the fact that new techniques and infrastructures are required for the sustainable exploitation of a huge amount of data. The Linked Data paradigm is often seen as an approach to coping with Big Data, as it moves the attention from a Web of documents to a Web of rich data.

Nevertheless, the great availability of resources raises data management issues, that must be faced in a dynamic, highly distributed, and heterogeneous environment, such as the Web: (i) how to model large amounts of (linked) data, (ii) how to query data and reason on them in a feasible way, (iii) how to exploit Big and Linked Data applications in real-world scenarios. To solve these issues means to exploit the synergism between the conceptual foundations of data management and logical foundations of Big and Linked Data initiatives. At the same time, emerging Big Data technologies could be useful in addressing data management issues within the Linked Data context. Among them, modern distributed technologies based on the principles of CAP theorem, such as NoSQL DBMS and Map/Reduce data processing.

This Special Issue collects four high-quality papers that aim at investigating Linked Data and Big Data interleaving issues under a data management perspective: (a) two papers propose the application of clustering techniques for performing inference and search over (linked) data sources; (b) a paper leverages graph analysis techniques to enable application-level integration of institutional data; (c) a paper describes an approach for protecting users' profile data from disclosure, tampering, and improper use.

January 2015

Devis Bianchini
Valeria De Antonellis
Roberto De Virgilio

Editorial Board

Contents

Structure Inference for Linked Data Sources Using Clustering

Klitos Christodoulou[(✉)], Norman W. Paton, and Alvaro A.A. Fernandes

School of Computer Science, University of Manchester,
Oxford Road, Manchester M13 9PL, UK
{christodoulou,norm,alvaro}@cs.man.ac.uk

Abstract. Linked Data (LD) overlays the World Wide Web of documents with a Web of Data. This is becoming significant as shown in the growth of LD repositories available as part of the Linked Open Data (LOD) cloud. At the instance-level, LD sources use a combination of terms from various vocabularies, expressed as RDFS/OWL, to describe data and publish it to the Web. However, LD sources do not organise data to conform to a specific structure analogous to a relational schema; instead data can adhere to multiple vocabularies. Expressing SPARQL queries over LD sources – usually over a SPARQL endpoint that is presented to the user – requires knowledge of the predicates used so as to allow queries to express user requirements as graph patterns. Although LD provides low barriers to data publication using a single language (i.e., RDF), sources organise data with different structures and terminologies. This paper describes an approach to automatically derive structural summaries over instance-level data expressed as RDF triples. The technique builds on a hierarchical clustering algorithm that organises RDF instance-level data into groups that are then utilised to infer a structural summary over a LD source. The resulting structural summaries are expressed in the form of classes, properties and, relationships. Our experimental evaluation shows good results when applied to different types of LD sources.

Keywords: Schema · Linked Data · Clustering · Query formulation

1 Introduction

In recent years there has been a significant growth in the amount of publicly available structured data on the Web using a graph-based representation model and a set of simple principles, the so-called *Linked Data Principles* [3]. A motivation for the adoption of these principles is the fact that they are based upon established web infrastructures (like URIs and HTTP) and semantic web standards (like RDF and RDFS), thus providing low barriers to data publication. The adoption of these principles is apparent in the number of Linked Data (LD) repositories that form the Linked Open Data (LOD) cloud[1]. An interesting aspect of this kind of Web is that datasets are not only published in isolation

---

[1] http://lod-cloud.net.

© Springer-Verlag Berlin Heidelberg 2015
A. Hameurlain et al. (Eds.): TLDKS XIX, LNCS 8990, pp. 1–25, 2015.
DOI: 10.1007/978-3-662-46562-2_1

but also interconnected with other datasets by the use of links. As the size of the LOD graph is constantly growing, with billion of triples publicly available from different domains, so does the need to consume data in this distributed environment.

Accessing the LOD cloud follows paradigms previously used for the web of documents. For example, various techniques from information retrieval are used by LD search engines (e.g., SWSE [10]) to support keyword queries. However, the web of data seems to provide the opportunity to move beyond keyword search queries into more precise query answering using structural queries. Often knowledge for answering a query is distributed across different datasets, so multiple queries need to be formulated and sent to more than one dataset for the user to get the desired answer. For the web of data this support is provided by SPARQL [18], the query language for RDF data sources. However, even though SPARQL supports querying over RDF sources it may still be difficult to formulate such queries. The basic building blocks for SPARQL queries require an understanding of how concepts are represented that may not be readily available. The fact that the RDF model [12] does not impose any constraints on the structure of a source makes it difficult to know what graph patterns can be formulated over a given source.

Evaluating structured queries over a LD repository that exposes its data as either a SPARQL endpoint or an RDF dump often requires the user to browse the source or to issue exploratory queries (e.g., Listing 1.1) in order to understand how the data are organised and what predicates are used to describe the entities. This, however, is time consuming and requires queries to be formed and asked manually. Although, it might be possible to browse a small RDF source, usually the knowledge as to how the data are organised in a source requires careful observation of the triples at the instance-level, which presents scalability challenges for browsing.

```
SELECT DISTINCT ?concept
WHERE {
    [ ] rdf:type ?concept .
}

SELECT DISTINCT ?concept ?prop
WHERE {
    ?s rdf:type ?concept .
    ?s ?prop ?v .
}
```

Listing 1.1. Exploratory SPARQL queries.

Generally, forming a meaningful query over a source is challenging without a structural summary of the underlying RDF source, therefore, it is important to have such an understanding. In relational databases, for instance, such an organisation of data is achieved using a logical schema to which data must adhere.

Such an organisation of data is not only useful for browsing the structure of the database but also for formulating queries or even capturing statistics that could enable query optimisation [6]. In contrast to the logical organisation imposed in relational databases, an RDF source does not conform to any analogous structure. In the context of LD, a schema of an RDF source is a combination of terms from various vocabularies that are used to represent the data, where their semantics are defined in various RDFS/OWL vocabularies [9].

Problem and Approach. It is often good practice for RDF datasets to provide a VoID[2] description that captures various metadata about a source. By retrieving such descriptions, users can get an idea about size statistics, which vocabularies are used in the source, which classes or predicates are used to describe the data, or how to access the source. Such descriptions however, lack sufficient structural metadata to provide a detailed description as to how the data is organised in a source. Typically, VoID descriptions are handcrafted by data publishers, and are not always available. As of August 2011, only 32.2 % of the LOD cloud data sources provided such descriptions[3]. In this paper we propose a technique based on cluster analysis that, by looking at instance-level data from an RDF source, can infer a structural summary (i.e., a schema) that captures information about *classes* that the data instantiate, their *properties* and how they relate to each other. Having such a structural summary over a source can be helpful in many application scenarios, such as for discovering sources, understanding the structure of a source, and supporting query formulation. Exploring such challenges is outside the scope of this paper.

Contributions. We note that the vision of distributed query processing over RDF sources can benefit from having structural summaries available for each source. At the same time we recognise that the low barriers to data publication introduced by the linked data principles must be preserved. We have proposed in our previous work [16] that pay-as-you-go data integration [5] can be used to enable distributed query processing over structurally heterogeneous and distributed LD sources. In such a context, there is a need to explore automatic techniques that support structure inference from RDF sources. With the work presented in this paper we take a step forward in this direction; our contributions are as follows:

- We have designed and implemented a technique that allows structural summaries to be inferred over RDF sources that contain explicitly stated instance-level data.
- We describe an experimental evaluation of the approach using different use-case scenarios that demonstrate its effectiveness.

In the remainder of this paper we begin by introducing a more formal definition of the problem in Sect. 2, followed by a detailed description of our technique in Sect. 3. We elaborate on the methodology used for evaluating the approach in Sect. 4, and we conclude in Sect. 6.

---

[2] See Vocabulary of Interlinked Datasets: http://www.w3.org/TR/void/.

[3] For more statistics, see http://www4.wiwiss.fu-berlin.de/lodcloud/state/.

2   Problem Description

By observing instance-level triples that are explicitly stated in a source, our aim is to have a synopsis of the sources. Following [1], we define an *RDF triple* as $(subject, predicate, object) \in (R \cup B) \times P \times (R \cup B \cup L)$, given a set of Resources R identified with URIs, a set of Blank Nodes B, a set of Predicates P and a set of Literals L. A set of RDF triples T forms an *RDF Graph*. Given T we are interested to derive a schema description as follows:

Definition 1. *A schema S is composed of a set of classes $\{C_1, ..., C_\mu\}$, where each $C_i (i = 1, ..., \mu)$ contains a set of predicates $\{C_i.P_1, ..., C_i.P_p\}$.*

As pointed out earlier, at the instance-level an RDF source does not conform to any specific structure that forces an organisation of the triples in the source and thus can be considered as schema-less. The data do not adhere to any explicit schema definition. The RDF model can describe resources with a mixture of terms from different vocabularies, where there is no restriction on the number of vocabularies or terms (i.e., predicates) used to describe a resource. Assume that the RDF graph T describes resources with the set of predicates P, where $|P| = J$. Then we define a description of a particular resource as a *Candidate Description*:

Definition 2. *A candidate description CD is a subset $P' \subseteq P$; the subset composed by a set of $j \leq J$ predicates of P.*

Given $\mathcal{CD}$, the set of all CDs, our target is to group (i.e., cluster) $\mathcal{CD}$ into k clusters, where k is computed through the algorithm described in Sect. 3.2. Our methodology will create a set of clusters $U = \{U_1, ..., U_k\}$, where $U_i \subseteq \mathcal{CD}$ $\forall$ $i = 1, ..., k$. Optimally all CD's in each U_i belong to the same *class*.

In brief, given an RDF graph, the technique looks for resource descriptions that are potential instances of the same *class* by looking at the predicates used to describe a resource and any RDF typing information available.

3   Method Description

In the following, we describe our technique for inferring a structural summary over an RDF source. Our approach is based on the assumption that we can identify recurring structural patterns of a possible concept by observing instance-level resource descriptions that are RDF triples. To detect such patterns we organise resource descriptions that are possible instantiations of a class together in groups using *cluster analysis*. Simply put, the idea of cluster analysis is to discover groups from a set of objects. These groups are known as *clusters* and a set of clusters is known as a *clustering*. The goal is to assign similar objects into the same cluster and separate them from clusters that contain objects which are not similar. Similarity between objects is measured by a distance function; more details on the clustering algorithm can be found on Sect. 3.2. From this point onwards we refer to objects as individuals and we represent them as candidate descriptions. Our technique uses a hierarchical clustering algorithm to detect groups among a pool of individuals that are *candidate descriptions* (as in Definition 2); each group identified as a result of the clustering algorithm can inform the identification of *classes* that instantiate data, their *properties* and their relationships to other classes. We use a toy example in Fig. 1 to describe our technique. The final inferred schema is represented by a simple Entity-Relationship (ER)

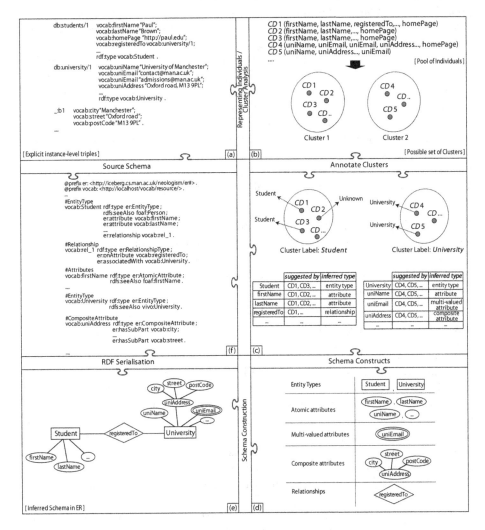

Fig. 1. (a) RDF triples represented with turtle (b) representation of individuals & clustering (c) annotation of clusters (d) explanation of inferred ER constructs (e) inferred schema represented as an ER diagram (f) inferred schema serialised as RDF-triples.

diagram where *classes* are represented as *entity types*, *properties* as *attributes* and *relationships* as *entity type relationships*.

3.1   Pre-processing

Initialisation. To gather instance-level information, the algorithm is presented with a SPARQL endpoint or an RDF dump. Figure 1(a) shows a snapshot of an RDF-graph represented in *turtle* notation. In the case of a SPARQL end-point, such information is obtained by posing SPARQL queries such as the ones shown in Listing 1.1. This is done to determine resources that are stated to be instantiations of some class by looking for RDF typing information (i.e., *rdf:type* statements). The resources that are determined as results of the queries are stored locally in a triple store. The flexibility of the RDF model does not impose any restriction on the use of *rdf:type* statements that determine whether a certain resource is an instantiation of some class. Thus we do not expect our simple heuristic to work for every RDF source. In case of an RDF dump we do not restrict the approach to resources that are instantiations of some class since the algorithm can look at all resources identified as being similar by the distance function and grouped in the same cluster, as we shall discuss later in Sect. 3.2. The RDF dump is imported into a local triple store that is used by the algorithm to access the resources.

Representing Individuals. Each resource identified with a unique URI is represented as a *candidate description* as in Definition 2. Examples of candidate descriptions are shown in Fig. 1(b). Having a pool of CDs, the algorithm proceeds to organise them into clusters using the clustering algorithm described in the following section.

3.2   Clustering Algorithm

To identify groups of similar instances, a hierarchical agglomerative clustering algorithm (as described in Algorithm 1) is used to group candidate descriptions into clusters. Our main criterion for choosing a hierarchical solution was the fact that we do not know in advance the appropriate number of clusters, and hierarchical clustering does not require any prior knowledge of this number. In non-hierarchical techniques, such as the k-means algorithms, the number of clusters needs to be specified in advance; this is in fact similar to deciding at which level to cut the final dendrogram in hierarchical clustering. Our approach uses the *silhouette coefficient* to determine the final number of clusters, as discussed in this section.

Typical hierarchical algorithms use a *similarity matrix* to cache the similarities of each pair of elements to be clustered. In our case the algorithm constructs a $|CD| \times |CD|$ similarity matrix that holds the pairwise similarities between clusters of CDs. To calculate the similarity between (CD_i, CD_j) the algorithm represents each CD as a set of features. For example, given the following candidate description $CD_1 = \{$vocab:firstName, vocab:lastName, vocab:homePage,

---

Algorithm 1. `Cluster Candidate Descriptions`

Require: Set of $\mathcal{CD} = \{CD_1, CD_2, ..., CD_{|CD|}\}$

1: $m \leftarrow 0$

2: $U^m \leftarrow \{\{CD_1\}, \{CD_2\}, ..., \{CD_{|CD|}\}\}$

3: Construct similarity matrix $M = |CD| \times |CD|$

4: Let (U_i^m, U_j^m) be the most similar pair in M:

5: $\underset{(U_i^m, U_j^m) \in M}{\operatorname{argmax}} \ cluster\_sim(\{U_i^m\}, \{U_j^m\})$

6: $max \leftarrow cluster\_sim(\{U_i^m\}, \{U_j^m\})$

7: **while** $(max \geq t)$ **do**

8:     $m \leftarrow m + 1$

9:     $U_{ij}^m \leftarrow U_i^{(m-1)} \cup U_j^{(m-1)}$

10:     $U^m \leftarrow (U^{(m-1)} \setminus \{U_i^{(m-1)}, U_j^{(m-1)}\} \cup U_{ij}^m)$

11:     $C \leftarrow C \cup U^m$

12:     Update similarity matrix M

13:     Let (U_i^m, U_j^m) be the most similar pair in M:

14:         $\underset{(U_i^m, U_j^m) \in M}{\operatorname{argmax}} \ cluster\_sim(\{U_i^m\}, \{U_j^m\})$

15:     $max \leftarrow cluster\_sim(\{U_i^m\}, \{U_j^m\})$

16: **end while**

17: **return** C

---

vocab: registeredTo} to find the set of features that characterises it we strip the namespace prefix from each predicate $p_j \in P'$. The output set of features will then be {firstName, lastName, homePage, registeredTo}. Let the function cd_sim (CD_i, CD_j) be the similarity measure between a pair of candidate descriptions where $i \geq 1, j \leq |CD|$. We then use the *Jaccard similarity coefficient* as the similarity measure, that is,

$$cd\_sim(CD_i, CD_j) = Jaccard(CD_i, CD_j) = \frac{|CD_i \cap CD_j|}{|CD_i \cup CD_j|} \in [0, 1]. \quad (1)$$

Having computed the similarity of each pair of CDs and stored it into the similarity matrix, the clustering algorithm proceeds as follows. Initially each CD is assigned to a singleton cluster. The algorithm keeps track of each iteration m by assigning a sequence number *0,1, ...,(m-1)* (Line 1). The set of clusters (i.e., clustering) produced at each iteration is denoted as U^m, thus by assigning each CD into its own cluster, $U^0 = \{\{CD_1\}, \{CD_2\}, ..., \{CD_{|CD|}\}\}$ (Line 2). In Lines 4 and 5 the algorithm identifies the most similar pair of clusters to be merged (according to our similarity measure). Then agglomerative hierarchical clustering proceeds iteratively (Line 6) by merging the *most similar* pair of clusters to form the next clustering $m = m + 1$ (Line 7) where $U_i^{(m-1)}$ and $U_j^{(m-1)}$ are the clusters. As a result of the merge step at each iteration m, the number of clusters decreases by one $|U^m| = |U^{(m-1)}| - 1$. The merge step produces a new cluster, $U_{ij}^m = U_i^{(m-1)} \cup U_j^{(m-1)}$ and clustering (Lines 8–9). In addition, at each step the algorithm stores each clustering (Line 10), to be used later as input for determining the best silhouette coefficient. Then the algorithm needs to update the similarities between the new (merged) cluster and the other clusters from the similarity matrix (Line 11). Numerous approaches have been developed for computing the similarity between two clusters [23]. For our algorithm we define the similarity between clusters U_i^m and U_j^m as the mean similarity between elements of each cluster (a.k.a average linkage),

$$cluster\_sim(U_i^m, U_j^m) = \frac{\sum\limits_{CD_a \in U_i^m} \sum\limits_{CD_b \in U_j^m} cd\_sim(CD_a, CD_b)}{|U_i^m||U_j^m|} \in [0,1]. \quad (2)$$

To compare the results of average linkage, we observed the results of running our clustering algorithm with other cluster similarity measures, such as:

- **Single Linkage:** The similarity between clusters U_i^m and U_j^m is calculated based upon the *maximal similarity* between elements of each cluster, defined as,

$$cluster\_sim(U_i^m, U_j^m) = \max_{CD_a \in U_i^m, CD_b \in U_j^m} cd\_sim(CD_a, CD_b). \quad (3)$$

- **Complete Linkage:** The similarity between clusters U_i^m and U_j^m is calculated based upon the *minimum similarity* between elements of each cluster, defined as,

$$cluster\_sim(U_i^m, U_j^m) = \min_{CD_a \in U_i^m, CD_b \in U_j^m} cd\_sim(CD_a, CD_b). \quad (4)$$

As discussed in Sect. 4.2, we have empirically determined that the above similarity schemes tend to give similar results. As for the termination condition, the algorithm stops when the most similar pair of clusters is below a certain threshold t, that is $cluster\_sim(U_i^m, U_j^m) < t$ (we elaborate on the choice of t in Sect. 4.2). To complete our discussion on the algorithm, by decreasing the number of clusters at each step the output (Line 15) is a sequence of clusterings.

Determining the Best Clustering. As explained in the previous section, several clusterings are produced by the algorithm (as depicted in Fig. 2(a)). Deciding which clustering best fits the data is a well known issue in cluster analysis [7], and approaches to solve this problem build on techniques that assess the quality of the clustering results. Usually such approaches determine the validity of a clustering based on the ideas of (a) *compactness*, i.e., how close the elements of a cluster are, and (b) *separation*, i.e., how distinct a cluster is from other clusters. We would like to keep our technique independent of any external information such as externally supplied class labels, thus we have used *silhouette coefficients* for evaluating the various clusterings (for more on clustering validation see [7]).

A silhouette coefficient (SC) is calculated for each individual and is a measure of how similar the individual is to other individuals in its own cluster compared to

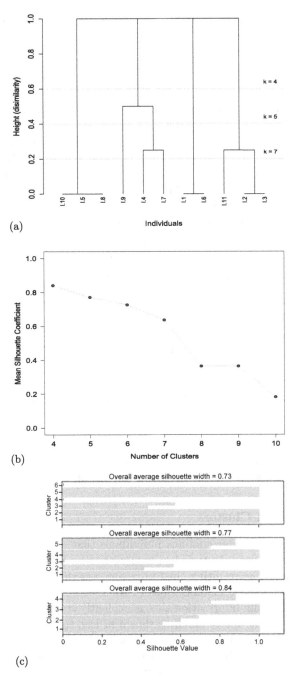

(a)

(b)

(c)

Fig. 2. (a) Hierarchical clustering result represented as a dendrogram with possible cut points, (b) shows the average silhouette coefficient for different clusterings, and (c) *silhouette-plot* that shows the silhouette coefficient calculated for each individual in each cluster.

other individuals from other clusters. Considering both cohesion and separation, the SC is defined as follows [11],

$$sil(i) = \frac{b(i) - a(i)}{max\{b(i), a(i)\}} \in [0, 1]. \tag{5}$$

Given an individual i in some cluster U, a(i) is the average dissimilarity[4] of i and all other individuals in cluster U and b(i) is the average dissimilarity between i and individuals of the closest cluster to U. We follow the definition by Kaufman and Rousseauw [11] which states that singleton clusters have $sil(i) = 0$. Having the silhouette values for each individual we can calculate the *average silhouette width* (ASW) for each cluster $ASW_{cluster}$ as the mean value of all $sil(i) \ \forall \ i \in U$ and the $ASW_{overall}$ for the entire population as the mean of all individual $sil(i)$ silhouettes. This is defined as,

$$ASW_{overall}(k) = \frac{\sum\limits_{i=1}^{n} sil(i)}{n} \in [0, 1], \tag{6}$$

where n denotes the number of all individuals. To determine the best clustering and thus the number of clusters k we choose the clustering with the highest $ASW_{overall}$. Using a dendrogram Fig. 2(a) visualises the outcome of running the clustering algorithm with possible cut points that give rise to different number of clusters, k. For each such clustering Fig. 2(b) shows the value of the silhouette coefficient for different number of clusters whereas in more detail Fig. 2(c) is a *silhouette plot* that shows the silhouette coefficient calculated for each individual in each cluster.

In our example, the clustering algorithm terminates when the dissimilarity between clusters is at the maximum (i.e., 1) and therefore there are no more clusterings produced fewer than 4, which also happens to be the clustering with the maximum silhouette coefficient; thus, $k = 4$ in this case.

3.3 Annotation of Clusters

Class Names. Each cluster contains individuals that are similar according to the distance measure used. In the ideal case all similar individuals are grouped in the same cluster. The resulting clustering suggests that individuals classified in some group are possible instantiations of some class. By observing the individuals, any RDF typing information that is explicitly stated is used to annotate each cluster with a descriptive label, as shown in Fig. 1(c). This label gives rise to the names of the classes we are looking to infer. We have used a greedy algorithm that suggests that the class label that occurs the most in a particular cluster is chosen as the class name. As our evaluation in Sect. 4 shows, this simple approach yields good results. In the case of clusters that contain individuals without *rdf:type* statements a special label, "Unknown" is used as the inferred

---

[4] Is the opposite of a similarity.

cluster label. One might then use the inference semantics of RDF graphs to infer the RDF typing information in cases where such information is not available. Finally, in cases where the clustering approach gives rise to different clusters that partition individuals of the same type, the technique will have to choose which cluster to use to infer a description for that class. A cluster with more of the individuals with that *rdf:type* stands a better chance of containing sufficient information that can guide the development of a schema, therefore the technique prefers such a cluster. We discuss this case in our evaluation in Sect. 4.3. To sum up, cluster labels represent the names of possible classes that organise data in an RDF source; examples are *Student* and *University* as shown in Fig. 1(c).

Class Properties. The formal definition of an *RDF triple* (see Sect. 2) suggests that an object could be either a literal, a blank node or a resource. The algorithm follows a simple heuristic and takes into consideration predicates that are literals to annotate a discovered class with its attributes. However, often resources have predicates that point to blank nodes. In such cases the algorithm considers blank nodes as evidence for identifying multi-valued or composite attributes for our ER model representation, as depicted in Fig. 1(d). We have also observed that the RDF model does not restrict resources, that are instantiations of the same class to have the same number of attributes. For example, a resource that is an instantiation of a class *Student* could use only predicates {firstName, last-Name, registeredTo, homePage} whereas another resource could be described using just {firstName, lastName, homePage}, omitting *registeredTo*. So as not to miss any attributes the algorithm takes the union of the predicate labels in the cluster as the list of identified attributes. For example, the *Student* class could have attributes {firstName, lastName, registeredTo, homePage}. In addition, this phenomenon of missing attributes could be due to cases of specialisation/-generalisation relationships. With this reflected upon the instances the algorithm chooses to union the properties identified in each cluster.

Class Relationships. To infer relationships between our identified class labels we observe predicates that are URI-links to other resources rather than literals. Simply put, we follow the heuristic: *an RDF triple that is a URI-link rather than a literal is a candidate relationship, and it is a relationship within the RDF graph if it refers to another entity within the same RDF graph.* For each identified class, by observing the predicates of its individuals, we extract all predicates that are candidate relationships according to our heuristic. This provides the algorithm with enough information to identify relationships for inferred classes.

3.4 Schema Constructs

The simple Entity-Relationship (ER) conceptual model is expressive enough to model our inferred schema, and we have used a simple set of mapping rules, to express our inferred structure using ER constructs. As shown in Fig. 1(d), inferred Classes are modelled as *entity types*, class properties that consist of single atomic values are modelled as *atomic attributes* whereas ones that occurred multiple times are considered as evidence of *multivalued attributes* and are modelled as such. Any properties that point to anonymous resources (i.e., a BNodes) are modelled as *composite attributes*, and finally any properties that point to other resources are modelled as *relationship types*. To depict the constructs of an inferred schema we have used the classic diagrammatic conventions of ER.

3.5 Schema Construction and Serialisation

Finally, having collected enough information to annotate entity types with attributes and relationships, the algorithm proceeds to infer a structural summary over the imported RDF source. Figure 1(e) shows a simple schema (represented as an ER-diagram) that has been inferred from a simple RDF source. To conform with the context of LD, we have used a simple RDFS vocabulary to serialise the inferred schema as RDF triples. To the best of our knowledge[5] there is no RDFS vocabulary that captures the constructs of the ER model. Thus, we have created one and published it using best practises suggested by the Linked Open Vocabularies (LOV) project, and then used it to serialise our inferred schema as an RDF graph (see Fig. 1(f)). To conclude, we have noticed that there are some attempts in the literature [4] to map ER diagrams to OWL ontologies. The outcome of our structure inference technique can be used as an input to such techniques.

4 Empirical Evaluation

In the following, we present the methodology used for evaluating our technique. To ensure diversity in the LD sources used for the evaluation we distinguish between two different types of RDF sources: those that have been generated by a translation from relational databases using a systematic approach (such as the D2RServer tool [2]) and real-world Linked Data sources from the Web of Data. We have categorised the sources into two groups according to their generation method, as in Table 1.

Table 1. Linked Data sources used for evaluation.

	Name	# triples	# classes	BNodes	generated_by
1	cdShop	303	3	Y	D2RServer
2	Conference	300	8	Y	D2RServer
3	BIRT_db[a]	28.5 k	8	N	D2RServer
4	Jamendo	1.1 M	11	N	DBTune.org
5	Magnatune	322 k	7	N	DBTune.org

[a]http://www.eclipse.org/birt/phoenix/db.

---

[5] Observing the vocabularies listed by the Linked Open Vocabularies (LOV) project: http://lov.okfn.org/dataset/lov/.

The RDF graphs that were used during the evaluation have been manually downloaded and imported into a local triple store since some of the datasets were not always accessible and some others were only published as RDF dumps. For the evaluation of our technique we are looking to investigate whether the individuals have been assigned to the actual classes according to some ground truth. In addition, we would like to establish the extent to which our technique can infer a structural summary of the LD sources by identifying the correct classes, their properties and their relationships.

4.1 Experimental Methodology and Metrics

As previously mentioned, for each of the following experiments we are looking to measure (a) how good the clustering solution is at grouping individuals, and (b) how well the approach has identified the correct entity types, attributes and relationships.

Quality of Clusterings. For measuring the quality of the clustering, we have used the *FScore measure* [14]. This measure required us to manually assign class labels to each individual to form the gold standard. Having the gold standard we proceed to compute the FScore measure as follows. For each particular class label L_r of size n_r and cluster C_i of size n_i, with n_{ri} being the number of individuals in cluster C_i that belong to L_r, we measure the FScore of this class and cluster, using,

$$FScore(L_r, C_i) = \frac{2 \times P(L_r, C_i) \times R(L_r, C_i)}{P(L_r, C_i) + R(L_r, C_i)} \in [0, 1], \qquad (7)$$

where, $P(L_r, C_i)$ is the precision value defined as n_{ri}/n_i, and $R(L_r, C_i)$ is the recall value defined as n_{ri}/n_r for the class L_r and cluster C_i. The FScore of the class L_r is the maximum FScore. To understand how good the choice of the determined clustering solution is we also calculate the overall FScore, using the following formula, where $|L|$ is the number of classes and n the number of individuals, that is,

$$Overall\_FScore = \sum_{r=1}^{|L|} \frac{n_r}{n} max(FScore(L_r, C_i)) \in [0, 1]. \qquad (8)$$

An ideal clustering solution is the one in which every class from the gold standard has a corresponding cluster where all the individuals of that class made it to the correct cluster, the higher the FScore the better the clustering.

Quality of Inferred Schemas. To measure how well our technique inferred schemas for LD sources we measure Precision/Recall and FScore for each of the ER constructs we are expecting (i.e., entity types, attributes and relationships). We have manually designed the schemas that we are expecting and compared them with the derived result. To design a gold standard, in cases that we had access to, we have observed the SQL schemas that populate a relational version of the data, otherwise we have just observed the resulting RDF-graphs.

For *entity-types* we determine true positives, i.e. entity types needed and inferred, false positives, i.e. entity types not needed but inferred, false negatives, i.e. entity types needed but not inferred. For *attributes* and special types of attributes (e.g., composite) we determine true positives, i.e. attributes needed and inferred as attributes to the correct entity type, false positives, i.e. attributes not needed on an entity type, but inferred, false negatives, i.e. missed attributes. Finally, for *binary relationships* we determine true positives, i.e. relationships inferred between the correct entity types, false positives, i.e. relationships incorrectly inferred between entity types, and false negatives, i.e. any relationships missed.

Before discussing the results of our experiments, note that in the description of the clustering algorithm in Sect. 3.2 the termination condition of the algorithm depends on what the algorithm considers as the minimum similarity value for which a pair of clusters is considered as a candidate for merging. Thus before discussing any results on measuring the effect of our schema inference technique we elaborate on the choice of the minimum similarity value for merging and then we elaborate on the choice of the cluster-to-cluster similarity scheme (i.e., average, single and complete linkage). For the experiments Sects. 4.3 and 4.4, we have used as in Sect. 4.2, values for the above parameters that we have empirically determined.

4.2 Determining Parameters

Min. Threshold for Merging. As explained in Sect. 3.2, the clustering algorithm clusters together individuals with similar features. At each iteration the algorithm selects the most similar pair of clusters to be merged. To characterise that a pair of clusters is similar enough to be merged we have used a threshold t, which is the minimum similarity value a pair of clusters should have, to be considered as a candidate for merging. In this section we elaborate on the choice of t, by observing its effect on the maximum average silhouette width, and thus on the quality of the clustering. In doing so we have run the algorithm with different values for t, iteratively increasing its value by 0.1 until $t = 1.0$. This is shown in Fig. 3 where we have run our experiment using sources 1, 2 and 3 from Table 1. As t varies closer to 1.0 the algorithm becomes stricter in the choice of clusters to be merged. This means that individuals that are not similar enough remain unclustered, thus causing the average silhouette width to decrease, for the reason that most of the individuals remain in their singleton clusters. This is reasonable since, from the definition of the silhouette coefficient [11], singleton clusters have a silhouette value of zero. Such drops are shown in Fig. 3 for sources 2 and 3 when t is around 0.4 and 0.5 respectively. The values of the max. average silhouette width seem to remain constant for choices of t closer to 0, for the reason that the algorithm is more flexible in merging clusters that are not so similar. Varying t closer to 0 allows more merge steps, thus more iterations until termination. For each merge step the algorithm calculates the maximum average silhouette width overall for the clustering, and therefore changing t does not always have an effect on choosing the maximum $ASW_{overall}$.

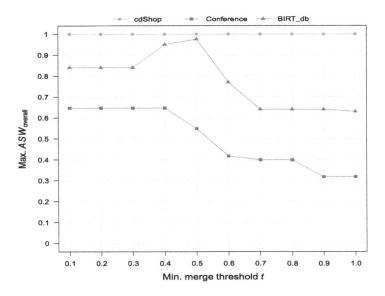

Fig. 3. Choice of t and its effect on the maximum average silhouette width.

Furthermore, in cases where most or all of the individuals from each class are using the same or almost the same set of predicates the choice of t does not seem to have any real effect, as in source 1. Because of the diversity of the data in the sources we cannot be very strict on the choice of t, however from this simple experiment it seems reasonable to choose a value for t to be in the range of $[0.4$–$0.5]$, therefore for the experiments to follow we choose $t = 0.5$.

Linkage Schemes. To complement our experiments on how good the clustering solution is, we have empirically observed the behaviour of the clustering algorithm using different linkage schemes for measuring the similarity between clusters (as mentioned in Sect. 3.2). For each of the RDF sources in Table 1, we have run the clustering algorithm and observed the effect of using a different scheme on the value of the silhouette coefficient. As shown in Fig. 4, in most cases the different schemes co-occur in identifying the number of clusters with the exception of *complete linkage*. As depicted in Fig. 4(b), using complete linkage the maximum average silhouette coefficient occurs when the number of clusters is 14 where the real number of clusters in the dataset is 9. On the other hand the alternative approaches are closer to identifying the real number of clusters. For our purposes it seems reasonable to choose single or average linkage because of their similar results, and in practise we have used the *average linkage* as the default linkage scheme.

4.3   Experiment 1: Reverse Engineering

Relational databases played a key factor in expanding the LOD cloud as a source for a large number of RDF triples. Tools like the D2R-Server [2] have been

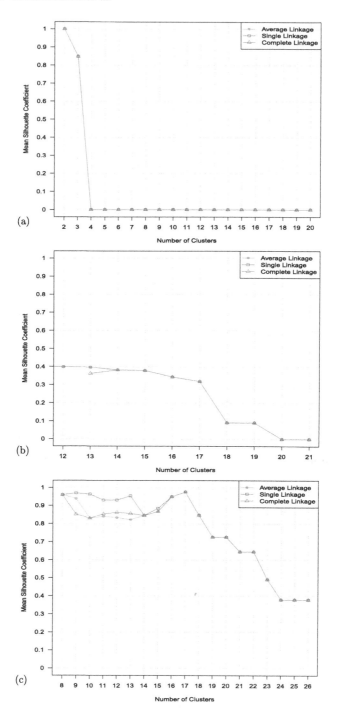

Fig. 4. Shows for each cluster similarity scheme, the top 10–20 occurrences of mean silhouette coefficient. x-axis shows the number of clusters in each clustering and y-axis the corresponding silhouette coefficient.

essential in providing a standardised way of exposing relational databases as LD sources on the Web. However, such datasets lack the organisation of a schema as previously existed in the relational database. With this experiment we are looking to demonstrate the effectiveness of our technique by reverse engineering the schema of some RDF sources that have been generated from a relational database (see Table 1). Before determining how well our technique inferred a schema, we would like to gain some insights regarding the quality of the clustering determined by the algorithm. This is important since our technique aims at looking for recurring patterns from the clusters formed, in order to infer the structure of the source. Figure 5(a) shows the result for a small dataset with only a few class labels. The algorithm has successfully assigned individuals to the correct clusters except those from the *Category* label. This was done intentionally by the algorithm since all instances of the Category class are represented as blank nodes in the RDF source. This evidence has been treated by the algorithm as a composite attribute, in our ER-model representation. This does not mean that the algorithm has missed the individuals of the Category class, instead, knowing the existence of a composite attribute we can easily formulate a SPARQL query to populate data from the Category class (e.g., Listing 1.2). The same also happened in Fig. 5(b) with a source that has more labels, however in this source some instances have not been classified in the correct classes. This is because the particular source has instances of different classes that use the same predicates. For example, *Researcher* and *PhDStudent* share {firstName, lastName, address, homePage}. Figure 5(c) shows the results for an RDF source with no blank nodes. The silhouette coefficient determined 17 clusters instead of 8 and therefore some individuals have not been assigned to any cluster, or individuals of the same type have been partitioned into several clusters. The choice of 17 clusters has been determined by the highest $ASW_{overall}$. For 17 clusters the average silhouette width is 0.976 and the second best, suggesting just 8 clusters is 0.960. However, the effect of the clustering produced by the SC does not influence the post-processing tasks downstream and as such the algorithm manages to get good results for the inferred structural summary (see Table 2).

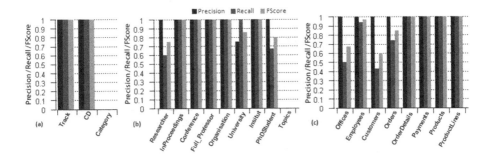

Fig. 5. Quality of the clustering solution.

To conclude this experiment, we observe how the quality of clustering influences the final inferred schema and the judgement of the algorithm in determining the schema of the source. Using the metrics described in Sect. 4.1 to evaluate the effectiveness of our technique, the results are presented in Table 2. For each of the sources we have compared the inferred schema results with the gold standard. The important observation is that the technique managed to infer a structure as expected with minor fallouts that influenced the performance.

Table 2. Evaluation of schema inference technique: (ET): Entity Types, (AT): Attributes, (R): Relationships

	cdShop			Conference			BIRT_db		
	ET	AT	R	ET	AT	R	ET	AT	R
Precision	1	1	1	1	1	1	1	1	1
Recall	1	1	1	1	0.90	0.86	1	0.92	0.86
FScore	1	1	1	1	0.95	0.92	1	0.96	0.92

In more detail, we have noticed that in all cases the algorithm manages to infer all the entity types (i.e., classes) that where expected. For classes that have resources as BNodes the algorithm creates a special type of attribute instead, thus we do not classify them as *false negatives*. Some instances translated from relational tables have NULL values in some of their attributes. Thus, there are cases where the algorithm misses some attributes. Regarding the identification of relationships between classes, the algorithm performs well. We have only noted some *false positives* in cases where classes participate in a class hierarchy. The algorithm is not aware of this and, therefore sometimes misplaces some of the relationships between different classes that participate in is-a relations. However, still the results are promising. We understand the diversity of LD sources in terms of representing data with different structures and terminologies, however, our prototype technique performed well in terms of inferring the structure of RDF sources that previously represented data as relational tables.

```
SELECT DISTINCT ?o ?category
WHERE {
    eShop:CdNo9 eShop:category ?o .
    ?o eShop:name ?category .
}
```

Listing 1.2. Explore *Category* class triples.

4.4   Experiment 2: On Sources from the Web of Data

We repeated the previous experiment on real sources from the LOD cloud that were not generated from existing schemas. For this experiment we have chosen

LD sources from *DBTune.org* namely *Jamendo* and *Magnatune*. Figure 6(a) shows the result from inferring the schema for *Jamendo*. In this source we have observed that some URI resources do not have any *rdf:type* statements therefore they have been classified as elements of our specialised "Unknown" class. Without any RDF typing information the label of the class cannot be determined. In such cases our technique creates several clusters labelled with the "Unknown" label. As already mentioned, the inference semantics of RDF graphs could provide an insight as to what could be a possible class label for our "Unknown" classes. Nevertheless, despite the lack of class label information the algorithm managed to infer the relationships and attributes for the "Unknown" class. Although this class has been inferred by the algorithm during our evaluation, we have considered it as a *false positive*, hence the decrease in the measures for Entity Types. Similarly, the relationships identified for the "Unknown" class are considered as *false positives*. This does not mean that the technique failed to determine the relationships as it should have, but it was unaware of the actual classes that participate in the relationship. Similarly, Fig. 6(b) depicts the results of running the algorithm over *Magnatune*. According to the gold standard designed for this source, the algorithm correctly inferred a structural description of the source as expected. We have noticed that, overall, the schemas of LD sources normally use a few classes to describe their resources and that the algorithm can perform well in inferring structural summaries over published LD sources.

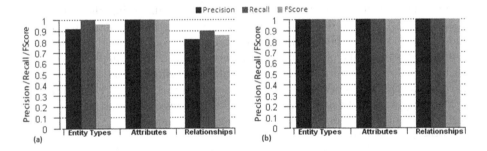

Fig. 6. Evaluation of schema inference technique.

5   Related Work

As already mentioned, the widespread adoption of the RDF model has led to an emerging need to access data from various heterogeneous and distributed data sources. Since the data are distributed, and due to the schema-less nature of the model, efficient retrieval of the data is a challenging task. In fact, several challenges contribute to this, some of which are: (i) the challenge of locating which datasets could possibly contribute answers to a given query, (ii) the lack of a comprehensive instance-level summary of the data, and (iii) scalability issues.

One approach to this challenge is based on *materialisation*, where a complete replica of the RDF graphs is stored in a central triple-store which is then used for query answering. However, such a central store assumes that the data remain static or evolve slowly, and that the most current version of the data is not required. Moreover, with the current size of the LD cloud, with more than 62 billion RDF triples[6], maintaining a replica is resource intensive, and the lack of an intensional description of the data makes query formulation a challenge. In this section we summarise ongoing research on proposals for solving some of the challenges related with efficient data management in the LOD ecosystem. We begin by discussing related work on locating datasets that can possibly contribute answers to a query, discovering RDF-specific schema knowledge from datasets and finally proposals on distributed query processing. We then position our work in relation to other proposals for discovering knowledge that can inform the formulation of SPARQL queries over a given RDF source.

On Source Discovery. There has been some recent research on source selection that provides summaries or descriptions of the RDF triples that can be found in LD sources using index structures [13,21]. We refer to these as *triple-level summaries*. An example of such work is *SchemEX* [13], which uses a stream-based approach for extracting schema information from RDF triples that are traversed from an RDF graph using a fixed-window. The extracted schema is then used to guide the construction of an index structure by linking schematic information to relevant datasets. Given a SPARQL query, SchemEX performs a lookup in the index structure to find which datasets contain instances of a specific RDF schema concept that can contribute to answering the query. As such, SchemEX aims to deal with the challenge of providing a summary of the kind of triples that can be found in a data source. By contrast, our work focuses on inferring a summary of how individuals are organised in a single source that can be used for query formulation, rather than on using the extracted schema for constructing an index that is used for relevant source discovery. In addition, both our approach and SchemEX utilise RDF typing information at the instance-level, aim to support query execution, and model the outcome of the extraction processes as RDF triples.

Harth, *et al.* [8] propose the use of an approximate multidimensional indexing structure (i.e., QTrees) as a data summary for determining which sources can potentially contribute answers to a query. The construction of an index structure is made possible by applying hash functions over the individual components of RDF triples (*subject, predicate, object*) contained in the datasets, to obtain data points that correspond to a three-dimensional QTree. A certain set of similar triples is then approximated by minimal bounding boxes (MBBs). At query time a set of MBBs is returned for each triple pattern in the query that suggest relevant sources that can contribute to the query result. Our work differs from the above approach since we would like to have an understanding of how concepts are represented in the sources and not a summary of what triples exist in which source. Thus the emphasis in [8], as exploited in [17], is on providing an

---

[6] http://stats.lod2.eu/.

instance-level summary that can inform efficient query evaluation, whereas the emphasis in our work is on providing a schema-level summary that can inform data integration.

On Knowledge Discovery and Ontology Mining. In a complementary approach, Zong, *et al.* [24] explored a method to dynamically generate a concept hierarchy using LD sources from the bio-medical domain. In doing so, their method utilises RDF typing information at the instance-level and builds upon hierarchical clustering. This is similar to our technique where a pre-processing step is necessary for determining the similarities between pairs of individuals using a distance function. The pair-wise similarities are then used as an input to the clustering step (as in Sect. 3). A similar work-flow is followed by their technique, where the similarity between a pair of individuals is measured over the predicate values that are *URIs*, whereas our technique computes the similarity by considering the local names of all predicates that are used in either *RDF-links* or *literal* triples. Despite the similarities, their approach builds on sources that use a single ontology to organise data, and is restricted in terms of dynamically identifying relationships between the inferred concepts, whereas in our proposal the discovery of domain/range axioms is made possible; captured as entity type relationships.

Another example of relevant work is from Völker, *et al.* [22], on mining ontologies from RDF data, an approach referred to as *Statistical Schema Induction*. In contrast to our technique that builds on clustering, their approach mines association rules from RDF data sources to acquire schema-level knowledge. Association rules that satisfy a user-provided confidence threshold contribute to the construction of the ontology. In our technique, the silhouette coefficient is used (as described in Sect. 3.2) to determine the clusters to be considered when inferring structural summaries. Finally, resources need to explicitly provide some RDF typing information for their approach to work. Although this is also useful for our technique, our approach is not as restricted since it organises resources into groups despite the existence of *rdf:type* statements and looks for recurring patterns that can guide the development of a schema.

Distributed Query Processing. Having an understanding of a schema can also support Distributed Query Processing (DQP) over RDF sources. DQP requires an understanding of how concepts are represented, but such information is typically not available for LD sources. Quilitz and Leser [19] propose *DARQ*, an engine for federated SPARQL queries. Transparent access to multiple SPARQL endpoints is provided by making use of hand-crafted source descriptions that summarise the URIs of RDF properties that are used by the source to describe the data. Our technique can provide similar structural summaries automatically. Rather than using indices of the content of each RDF source or statistical information (e.g., VoiD) FedX [20] does not require any metadata upfront; instead, it uses SPARQL ASK queries for source selection at query time to annotate triple patterns in the query with relevant sources, and relies on join order heuristics for efficient SPARQL query processing over several LD sources. Our approach suggests that structural summaries that can be used to inform query formulation can inferred automatically.

6   Conclusions and Future Work

This paper described a technique that uses a hierarchical agglomerative clustering approach and a set of simple heuristics to determine a structural summary over RDF sources, with the aim of informing query formulation and supporting query processing over LD sources. We have shown that having a schema for an RDF source that can be inferred automatically does not contradict the schema-free nature of RDF sources. The flexibility of the RDF model is preserved since we are not forcing the data to adhere to any specific structure; the data are just used to guide the creation of such structural summaries over the sources. In addition, having a structural summary over LD sources aligns with recent trends on publishing datasets that are annotated with metadata, such as VoID descriptions. We propose to organise individuals into clusters which can then used to search for recurring patterns, with the aim of inferring structural summaries over LD sources. Our empirical evaluation over sources that have been constructed from a direct translation from relational databases as well as on real sources from the Web of Data validated that our technique generates good results.

While our results are promising, there remain several challenges to be further explored. In the following we attempt to highlight some of these challenges along with possible solutions on how to improve our structural inference technique:

Identification of class hierarchies. Our evaluation revealed two cases where it might be possible for the approach to determine subsumption relations. Discovering class hierarchies can be an important feature of the approach, we discuss it here with an abstract example however we leave this feature as a potential future work. Let us assume the existence of a single cluster c_1 that does not overlap with any other cluster and that the set of individuals of c_1 suggest more that one class label for the cluster. This might be possible when individuals, that potentially belong to different concepts, end up in the same cluster c_1 for the reason that they are using the same set of predicates to describe their data but have different RDF typing information. Another possible case for observing potential subsumption relations is when clusters overlap. Assume the existence of two overlapping clusters c_1 and c_2, where, some individuals belong to both clusters, this is the set given by their intersection $c_1 \cap c_2$. Potentially a simple heuristic based on counts can determine `is-a` relations, we leave this feature and its evaluation as a possible future direction for improving the presented technique.

Lack of *RDF typing* information. It is often the case that RDF sources do not explicitly state *rdf:type* information for every resource that appears in the source, in fact, there might exist cases of RDF sources which entirely neglect such information. As previously discussed, RDF typing information is useful for our technique, however, the lack of such knowledge causes the technique to assign the specialised "Unknown" label to discovered classes. Ideas to discover additional knowledge that can assist our approach into discovering a suitable class label in such cases are, among others, *(i)* to utilise the inference semantics of RDF sources with the use of a reasoner [15] that is used over the explicitly stated RDF data to reveal more knowledge, including RDF typing information, that could be utilised by our technique, and *(ii)* to take advantage of the dereference capabilities of predicate URIs to obtain access to their semantics as specified in semantic web ontologies described in RDFS/OWL. For instance, the semantics of *rdfs:domain* as appeared in the definition of properties can suggest that a particular instance is a member of some class. Further investigation of these proposals is left as a future work.

Distance function. In Sect. 3.2 we discuss a simple distance function based on the use of *Jaccard similarity* over localnames of predicates to determine the pairwise similarities between individuals. There might be cases where localnames alone provide insufficient knowledge for suggesting a similarity between a pair of candidate descriptions. In the simplest case of introducing typos in localnames the current distance function will not be able to determine any similarity. For example, the Jaccard similarity between $\{firstName, lastName, homePage\}$ and, $\{frsName, lstName, hmPage\}$ produces zero, which is unacceptable. It is also quite frequent in complex LD sources that predicates from different vocabularies are using identical localnames. Such cases will cause our distance function to derive a misleading conclusion on judging that they are identical. The design of a distance function that overcomes such weaknesses is desirable. This is important for our approach since the pairwise similarities are the foundations on which the clustering algorithm is making its decisions; into forming the right clusters that will then give rise to possible classes, properties and relationships. An improved distance function can perhaps consider several sources of evidence for judging the similarity of a pair of individuals. A possible suggestion is to take into account the predicate values of triples that are RDF-links (i.e., triples that their object's values are URIs). Again, in cases where is possible, dereferencing predicate URIs may reveal additional semantic evidence that could be used as additional knowledge for judging their similarity. Finally, to deal with typos a syntactic distance metric such as edit-distance could be used. We leave the design of an improved distance function that considers the above suggestions and its evaluation as a future direction.

Acknowledgement. Klitos Christodoulou has been supported by funding from the UK Engineering and Physical Sciences Research council, whose support we are pleased to acknowledge.

References

1. Arenas, M., Gutierrez, C., Pérez, J.: Foundations of RDF databases. In: Tessaris, S., Franconi, E., Eiter, T., Gutierrez, C., Handschuh, S., Rousset, M.-C., Schmidt, R.A. (eds.) Reasoning Web. LNCS, vol. 5689, pp. 158–204. Springer, Heidelberg (2009)
2. Bizer, C., Cyganiak, R.: D2r server - publishing relational databases on the semantic web. In: 5th International Semantic Web Conference, p. 26 (2006)
3. Bizer, C., Heath, T., Berners-Lee, T.: Linked data - the story so far. Int. J. Semant. Web Inf. Syst. **5**(3), 1–22 (2009)
4. Fahad, M.: Er2owl: generating owl ontology from er diagram. In: Shi, Z., Mercier-Laurent, E., Leake, D. (eds.) Intelligent Information Processing IV. IFIP, vol. 288, pp. 28–37. Springer, Heidelberg (2008)
5. Franklin, M.J., Halevy, A.Y., Maier, D.: From databases to dataspaces: a new abstraction for information management. SIGMOD Rec. **34**(4), 27–33 (2005)
6. Goldman, R., Widom, J.: Dataguides: enabling query formulation and optimization in semistructured databases. In: Proceedings of the 23rd International Conference on Very Large Data Bases, pp. 436–445. Morgan Kaufmann Publishers Inc. (1997)
7. Halkidi, M., Batistakis, Y., Vazirgiannis, M.: On clustering validation techniques. J. Intell. Inf. Syst. **17**(2–3), 107–145 (2001)
8. Harth, A., Hose, K., Karnstedt, M., Polleres, A., Sattler, K.-U., Umbrich, J.: Data summaries for on-demand queries over linked data. In: WWW, pp. 411–420 (2010)
9. Heath, T., Bizer, C.: Linked Data: evolving the web into a global data space. In: Synthesis Lectures on the Semantic Web. Morgan & Claypool Publishers (2011)
10. Hogan, A., Harth, A., Umbrich, J., Kinsella, S., Polleres, A., Decker, S.: Searching and browsing linked data with swse: the semantic web search engine. J. Web Sem. **9**(4), 365–401 (2011)
11. Kaufman, L., Rousseeuw, P.J.: Finding Groups in Data: An Introduction to Cluster Analysis. Wiley-Interscience, New York (1990)
12. Klyne, G., Carroll, J.J.: Resource description framework (RDF): concepts and abstract syntax. Technical report, W3C (2004)
13. Konrath, M., Gottron, T., Staab, S., Scherp, A.: Schemex - efficient construction of a data catalogue by stream-based indexing of linked data. J. Web Sem. **16**, 52–58 (2012)
14. Larsen, B., Aone, C.: Fast and effective text mining using linear-time document clustering. In: KDD, pp. 16–22 (1999)
15. Ravi Bhushan Mishra and Sandeep Kumar: Semantic web reasoners and languages. Artif. Intell. Rev. **35**(4), 339–368 (2011)
16. Paton, N.W., Christodoulou, K., Fernandes, A.A.A., Parsia, B., Hedeler, C.: Pay-as-you-go data integration for linked data: opportunities, challenges and architectures. In: Proceedings of the 4th International Workshop on Semantic Web Information Management, SWIM 2012, pp. 3:1–3:8. ACM (2012)
17. Prasser, F., Kemper, A., Kuhn, K.A.: Efficient distributed query processing for autonomous RDF databases. In: Proceedings of the 15th International Conference on Extending Database Technology, EDBT 2012, pp. 372–383. ACM (2012)
18. Prud'hommeaux, E., Seaborne, A.: SPARQL query language for RDF. W3C Recommendation **4**, 1–106 (2008)
19. Quilitz, B., Leser, U.: Querying distributed RDF data sources with SPARQL. In: Bechhofer, S., Hauswirth, M., Hoffmann, J., Koubarakis, M. (eds.) ESWC 2008. LNCS, vol. 5021, pp. 524–538. Springer, Heidelberg (2008)

20. Schwarte, A., Haase, P., Hose, K., Schenkel, R., Schmidt, M.: FedX: optimization techniques for federated query processing on linked data. In: Aroyo, L., Welty, C., Alani, H., Taylor, J., Bernstein, A., Kagal, L., Noy, N., Blomqvist, E. (eds.) ISWC 2011, Part I. LNCS, vol. 7031, pp. 601–616. Springer, Heidelberg (2011)
21. Umbrich, J., Hose, K., Karnstedt, M., Harth, A., Polleres, A.: Comparing data summaries for processing live queries over linked data. World Wide Web **14**(5–6), 495–544 (2011)
22. Völker, J., Niepert, M.: Statistical schema induction. In: Antoniou, G., Grobelnik, M., Simperl, E., Parsia, B., Plexousakis, D., De Leenheer, P., Pan, J. (eds.) ESWC 2011, Part I. LNCS, vol. 6643, pp. 124–138. Springer, Heidelberg (2011)
23. Zhao, Y., Karypis, G.: Evaluation of hierarchical clustering algorithms for document datasets. In: CIKM, pp. 515–524 (2002)
24. Zong, N., Im, D.-H., Yang, S.-K., Namgoong, H., Kim, H.-G.: Dynamic generation of concepts hierarchies for knowledge discovering in bio-medical linked data sets. In: Proceedings of the 6th International Conference on Ubiquitous Information Management and Communication, ICUIMC 2012, pp. 12:1–12:5. ACM (2012)

The Web Within: Leveraging Web Standards and Graph Analysis to Enable Application-Level Integration of Institutional Data

Luiz Gomes Jr.[(✉)] and André Santanchè

Institute of Computing, University of Campinas (UNICAMP),
Campinas, SP 13083-852, Brazil
{gomesjr,santanche}@ic.unicamp.br
http://www.ic.unicamp.br

Abstract. The expansion of the Web and of our capacity of producing and storing information have had a profound impact on the way we organize, manipulate and share data. We have seen an increased specialization of database back-ends and data models to respond to modern application needs: text indexing engines organize unstructured data, standards and models were created to support the Semantic Web, Big Data requirements stimulated an explosion of data representation and manipulation models. This complex and heterogeneous environment demands unified strategies that enable data integration and, especially, cross-application, expressive querying.

Here we present a new approach for the integration of structured and unstructured data within organizations. Our solution is based on the Complex Data Management System (CDMS), a system being developed to handle data typical of complex networks. The CDMS enables a relationship-centric interaction with data that brings many advantages to the institutional data integration scenario, allowing applications to rely on common models for data querying and manipulation.

In our framework, diverse data models are integrated in a unifying RDF graph. A novel query model allows the combination of concepts from information retrieval, databases, and complex networks into a declarative query language that extends SPARQL. This query language enables flexible correlation queries over the unified data, enabling support for a wide range of applications such as CMSs, recommendation systems, social networks, etc. We also introduce *Mappers*, a data management mechanism that simplifies the integration of heterogeneous data and that is integrated in the query language for further flexibility. Experimental results from real data demonstrate the viability of our approach.

Keywords: Query model integration · Data integration · DB/IR Integration · Graph data models · Graph query languages · Complex data

1 Introduction

Digital data availability has grown to unprecedented levels and surpassed our capacity of storage and analysis. This has led to the Big Data and NoSQL

© Springer-Verlag Berlin Heidelberg 2015
A. Hameurlain et al. (Eds.): TLDKS XIX, LNCS 8990, pp. 26–54, 2015.
DOI: 10.1007/978-3-662-46562-2_2

movements, aiming at tackling the increasing demands for scalability. A parallel development regards the proportional increase in data complexity. Capturing and processing greater amounts of data produces information that is correlated in diverse and intricate ways. Furthermore, recent developments in processing power, modeling, and algorithms enable the implementation of systems that better explore the increased complexity of data. All these factors influenced and enabled the dissemination of social networks and initiatives like the Linked Open Data[1].

Realizing the potential of the relationships inside the interconnected data and developing the means for their analysis fueled the development of the areas of complex networks [11] and link mining [14]. Related techniques have been applied in several scenarios, such as systems biology, neuroscience, communication, transportation, power grids, and economics [10].

In this article we aim to show how the focus on relationship analysis is important for institutional data and applications. Assessing properties of how data is correlated is the basis for several tasks, such as document retrieval, item recommendation and entity classification. We, therefore, advocate the vision that institutional data can be seen as a big complex network and, most importantly, several modern and commonplace applications can be specified in terms of link analysis tasks. A unified, relationship-centric framework for data and applications can enable a new level of integration, encompassing data from diverse sources (e.g. structured and unstructured) and applications (e.g. information retrieval, machine learning, data mining). This application-level integration allows developers to rely on common models for data interaction, simplifying development of applications with information needs that span multiple querying paradigms.

Institutional data and applications have, however, several requirements that make it hard to apply link mining techniques directly. The size of the data, its dynamic nature, and heterogeneity are not considered in traditional approaches. The focus of complex network techniques is typically on homogeneous networks with a single type of relationship (e.g. social networks), employing off-line algorithms to assess snapshots of the data. Modern applications, on the other hand, favor online access to subsets of the data, and must handle data heterogeneity seamlessly.

Here we introduce the Complex Data Management System (CDMS), which aims at providing query-based interaction for complex data. The proposed query model allows users to specify information needs related to the topology of the correlations among data. It also offers management mechanisms that are more adequate to the increased importance of the relationships in the data.

The increased expressiveness in the new framework provides a better match to the requirements in the described institutional settings. The online query mechanism allows the composition of queries that explore diverse aspects of how data is correlated. This not only allows the same query model to be used in diverse application scenarios, but also allows queries that encompass concepts

---

[1] http://www.w3.org/standards/semanticweb/data.

from multiple paradigms and data sources, such as in queries like "retrieve documents related to the keyword query 'US elections' and the topic *politics*, written by democrat journalists, ranked by relevance to the keyword query and reputation of the author".

To enable this type of interaction, the underlying institutional data must be integrated. Here we describe how we are fostering web standards to enable the required integration. Once the data is integrated, the CDMS is used to provide the proposed querying infrastructure. To tackle the integration of data models, we employ an RDF graph that interconnects data from diverse sources and models. The flexibility of graph models allows easy mapping from otherwise incompatible models (e.g. unstructured text and structured databases). Figure 1 contextualizes the elements in our proposal: several data sources are integrated in a unifying graph, which allows our framework to enable a more expressive interaction between users and data.

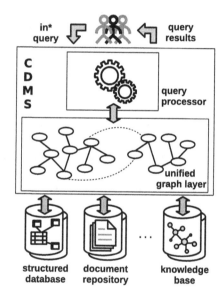

Fig. 1. Architecture of a CDMS deployed in a data integration scenario

As for integration at the query and application level, we acknowledge the importance of the Information Retrieval (IR) and Databases (DB) fields – which dominate data-driven applications in current settings – and describe how our new query model, which leverages complex network analysis, unifies concepts from these areas. To enable our query model over the unifying graph, we reinterpret querying concepts from diverse areas into graph analysis tasks. We implement this model in a new query language called in* (in star), which is an extension grammar for existing languages such as SPARQL.

We also address architectural issues related to the integration process, introducing the concept of *mappers*, which aim at simplifying relationship management. Mappers are similar to *stored procedures* in databases, triggered when nodes are created to carry customized tasks such as adding appropriate relationships or even other new nodes. Our *mappers* are integrated in the query model for further flexibility.

We aim at contributing towards a more unified and expressive interaction between users and data through this relationship-centric querying and data management framework. Experiments with real data are presented to demonstrate the expressiveness and practicability of our framework.

This paper is organized as follows: Section 2 discusses the new challenges for the current heterogeneous technological landscape. Section 3 introduces the Complex Data Management System, which is the basis for our integration approach. Section 4 describes the requirements for data access and model integration in our framework as well as issues related to query model integration, a fundamental concept in our proposal. Section 5 details our integrated query model and discusses usage scenarios. Section 6 introduces related data management issues and describes our *mapper* mechanism. Section 7 demonstrates experiments for our query language and the use of mappers in scenarios based on a large and interlinked database of movies. Section 8 contextualizes related work in respect to our proposal. Finally, Sect. 9 concludes the paper.

2   New Challenges for Institutional Data and Application Integration

The new scenario of overwhelming accumulation of information has a profound impact on the way we organize and manipulate data. We have seen an increased specialization of database back-ends and data models to respond to modern application needs: text indexing engines organize data on the Web, standards and models were created to support the Semantic Web, Big Data requirements stimulated an explosion of data representation and manipulation models labeled under the NoSQL umbrella. This complex and heterogeneous environment demands unified strategies that enable data integration and, more importantly, cross-application, expressive querying.

Although data integration has been an active research topic for many decades, most proposals depart from environments that do not take into account the modern diversity of technological infrastructures. Federated databases, for example, usually adopt the relational model to integrate data sources, with limited capabilities when dealing with semi or unstructured data. Similarly, in typical OLAP implementations, the benefits of integration are restricted by the adopted query model: data analysts may answer complex questions, but there is no direct benefit to other applications inside the institution. For example, Web developers cannot leverage the potential of the integration in their implementations of recommendation systems because they typically work on very different query models. Similar issues also appear in other contexts, such as the Semantic Web, which brings great benefits for data integration but querying capabilities do not match the diversity of Web applications.

A level of integration that covers a wide range of data models and, more importantly, data query models would not only allow applications to incorporate more relevant information, but would also allow more expressive queries that combine elements from different querying paradigms. For example, consider the following queries:

- retrieve documents related to the keyword query "US elections" and the topic *politics*, written by democrat journalists, ranked by relevance to the keyword query and reputation of the author;
- retrieve employees relevant to a given project ranked by their reputation among peers;
- retrieve profiles of people over 30 years old, ranked by similarity of hobbies on their profiles to hobbies on my own;
- retrieve products not yet purchased by the client Bob that are relevant to him.

These queries cover a broad range of data models (e.g. unstructured documents, relational, graph) and applications (CMSs, social networks, recommendation systems). The queries also combine concepts from diverse query models, such as relational predicates, keywords, ranking, and metrics of relevance and reputation. These and similar queries show up in many situations in typical institutions, both for internal, administrative purposes or for Web applications developed for external use. Answering these queries in current infrastructures typically demands substantial amount of resources and engineering to design ad-hoc subsystems.

To provide an overarching approach for querying, data model integration and query model integration must be tackled simultaneously. Querying is especially challenging, given the diversity of the data and the complexity of the information needs. The central observation underlying this article is that these issues can be mapped into complex network analysis tasks. Several tasks typically associated with the information retrieval and machine learning fields – including document retrieval, recommendation, and classification – draw inferences from how information pieces are correlated. Even though the correlations are often not explicit, it is intuitive to consider the data as a graph and notice the importance of the relationships and the underlying topology for each task. Our hypothesis is that an expressive query model that can capture topological properties in query time can be used to integrate these information needs in a single conceptual framework. We aim to show how the CDMS can be used in these scenarios, providing expressive querying and data management mechanisms that are appropriate to the heightened importance of relationships in the described scenarios.

3   Complex Data Management

The database framework used in our proposal is being developed to tackle issues associated with Complex Networks. In a complex network [11], the patterns defined by the interconnections are non-trivial, deviating substantially from cases where connections have the same probability (e.g. lattices or random graphs). The techniques developed for complex network analysis have become important resources in diverse fields such as systems biology, neuroscience, communication, transportation, power grids, and economics [10]. These areas deal with complex structures that requires specific techniques for analysis. In all cases, relationship analysis is a major aspect for knowledge acquisition. Typically, these structures generate emergent behavior, which are determined by the complex interactions among their simple constituent elements.

As a result of increased capacity of data storage and processing, these scenarios have come forth in other areas, such as enterprise data management, our focus on this paper. A typical institution nowadays stores and processes many textual documents alongside traditional structured data, communication and transaction records, and fast changing data about market and competition. These data are highly interlinked, by design or through intricate (and potentially imprecise) data analysis procedures such as named entity recognition, sentiment analysis, and recommendation systems.

Our CDMS is aimed at enabling querying and management of what we define as *complex data*. Complex data is characterized when relationships are central to data analysis. In these cases, the graph formed by data entities (nodes) and relationships (links) present properties typical of complex networks. The CDMS is aimed at providing adequate support for handling and querying complex data. It differs from typical DBMSs in four main aspects: (i) data model, (ii) query language, (iii) query evaluation, and (iv) data management mechanisms. Each of these items is described below.

- **Data model:** The data in target CDMS applications typically do not comply to pre-defined schemas. The high number and diversity of the relationships require a model where relationships are first-class citizens. Graph models are obvious choices in these settings. Their flexible modeling characteristics enable easy mapping of most types of data. Nodes with immediate access to neighbors is also an important feature for the type of computation involved. The CDMS framework adopts weighted edge-labeled property multigraphs to encode complex data. In this article, we leverage the RDF model to integrate institutional data.
- **Query language:** Our CDMS query language is intended to be flexible enough to allow correlation of data when little is known about how they are linked and organized. We developed a declarative query language that extends existing graph languages by introducing ranking based on a set of flexible correlation metrics. The ranking metrics proposed are: relevance, connectivity, reputation, influence, similarity, and context. The proposed language is designed as an extension for existing graph languages. In this article we show how SPARQL can be extended to enable the new query model.
- **Query evaluation:** Our abstractions for query evaluation fully support the query language while allowing for under-the-hood optimizations. We adopt a variation of the spreading activation (SA) model as our main abstraction for

query evaluation. The model allows the specification of the ranking metrics that are the basis of our query language. The SA mechanism is based on traversing the network from a initial set of nodes, activating new nodes until certain stop conditions are reached. By controlling several aspects related to this activation flow, it is possible to infer and quantify the relationships of the initial nodes to the reached ones.

- **Data management mechanisms:** Relationship creation is an important and defining operation for the described application scenarios. For example, several text indexing tasks, such as topic modeling, derive relationships between the text and more general concepts. In machine learning applications, elements are associated with features or classification categories, for example. In our framework, the creation of relationships is encapsulated in mappers. Mappers are very similar to *stored procedures*. What sets them apart are (i) their integrated use in our ranking queries, and (ii) how they are hooked in the databases's API so that any new data that matches the mapping criterion is passed through appropriate mappers.

The CDMS offers an architecture where relationships are central elements of the database. It enables queries to tap into properties derived from topological characteristics of the underlying graph. CDMS's new query model and management mechanisms allow for new levels of expressiveness for several tasks, simplifying integration of data from diverse sources and allowing distinct applications to employ the same query model over the integrated data.

4   Data and Query Model Integration

The level of integration that we aim at requires solutions to three main issues: (i) unified data access, so that queries have access to all data, (ii) unified data model, so that queries can reference data from diverse formats; and (iii) unified query model, so that applications can have a single interface for interaction with data. This level of integration allows applications to be based on the same underlying models to interact with data, what we call application-level integration.

4.1   The Local Unified Graph

Institutions face similar challenges to that of the Web: data produced by diverse groups in distinct contexts must be integrated to allow for more capable and outreaching applications. Although several research and products were developed to address these issues, we argue that revisiting this problem through the perspective of the new developments in applications and standards of the Web would allow for a more adequate interaction with modern institutional data.

The Semantic Web initiative has advertised the benefits of treating the Web as an integrated Giant Global Graph (GGG) [5]. Similar benefits could be achieved inside institutions by integrating all their data in a Large Local Graph (LLG). A LLG lacks the diversity and magnitude of the GGG, but it allows higher levels of control over data and local processing power, enabling better semantic integration among distinct data sources and more expressive querying. Another advantage of creating LLGs is that it facilitates transference of information to and from the GGG.

The framework proposed here assumes an underlying LLG. Although our solutions have interesting applications also in the context of the Semantic Web, we require levels of integration and processing power that are not currently available for the GGG. We, therefore, focus on institutional data but expect that in the future technological advances would allow similar interactions in a broader context.

A LLG is meant to integrate a broad range of data from an institution. Aggregation of external data from the GGG would also be important in many scenarios. Integrating data across domains and models is important to allow rich correlation queries between diverse data elements. The graph model is suiting for this scenario. Its simplicity and flexibility allows the representation of most of the popular data models [3,6]. Figure 2 shows a graph containing data derived from documents and relational databases (more details on the mapping in Sect. 4.2).

Here we employ the RDF(S) model for the LLG for several reasons: it is a stable and popular model, it implements a flexible graph model, classes facilitate the mapping of other models (e.g. object, relational), integration with other standards (e.g. URI, XML), standardized query language (SPARQL), simplified data sharing, etc.

It is important to emphasize that the strategy to create the unified graph is environment-specific. Although we provide general guidelines on how data should be represented as nodes and edges, our framework assumes the data are converted and interlinked in a coherent graph. What we want to show in this paper, and our main contribution, is that popular query models can also be translated into graph concepts, employing graph analysis in query processing. To take full advantage of the model, users should be aware of the semantics of the elements composing the graph. In that regard, our strategy is similar to an OLAP environment, in which the query model assumes data are integrated in a multidimensional schema – according to whichever strategy is adequate for the specific environment.

4.2   Data Model Integration

There are several alternatives for mapping a given data model into graphs. Although our framework works independently of the strategy adopted, we provide guidelines on basic transformations of typical models.

Here we focus on the integration of text documents and the relational model. The mapping for other models, such as semi-structured or NoSQL variations, can be derived by similar approaches. There are several alternatives for mapping a relational scheme to an RDF graph [3,6]. There is even a W3C working group[2] to define standards for these mapping languages. Here, to simplify the

---

[2] http://www.w3.org/2001/sw/rdb2rdf/.

discussion, we assume that (i) table descriptions become RDF classes, (ii) rows become instances of their respective tables, with their primary keys as identifiers, (iii) columns become properties of the instances, with values corresponding to literals and foreign keys becoming explicit links to other instances.

Graph representation of documents for IR purposes is also possible. An inverted index (in the bag of words model) can be readily mapped into a graph that connects terms and documents. More modern schemes to index documents such as topic models [8] and explicit semantic analysis [25] also fit nicely into this strategy, bringing the benefits of reduced dimensionality (i.e. avoiding creating an unnecessarily large graph containing entire postings list), less semantic ambiguity, and more cognitive appeal.

In our framework, a keyword query is also represented as a (temporary) node in the graph. The same indexing strategy used for the stored documents is applied to generate the relationships of the query node (Fig. 2). This graph representation of keyword queries allows them to be expressed alongside structured predicates in the queries (Sect. 5.3).

To simplify data management in the complex integrated graphs, our framework introduces mappers. Mappers play an important role in data model integration, being the mechanism that encapsulates the creation of relationships between elements of the graph.

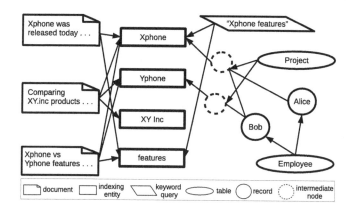

Fig. 2. Data elements represented as a unified graph

Figure 2 shows a simplified example to illustrate diverse elements represented as a unified graph. News articles about products are mapped into entities according to mappers that implement an indexing/annotation technique (e.g. topic modeling, named entity recognition, etc.). A keyword query is likewise mapped into these entities, using the same mapper in query time. Relational data from tables (Project, Employee) are also mapped into nodes in the graph and also connected to the entities. More details on the use of mappers to bridge data models are presented in Sect. 6.

4.3 Query Model Integration

Data access and model integration brings many benefits to institutions, providing a unified path for interaction with data. This interaction is, however, usually constrained by the data model and the query language employed for the integration. For example, in a typical OLAP setting, data are integrated in a data warehouse, but no direct benefit is gained by applications such as institutional search engines. The problem is that there is a conceptual gap between the interaction language in the integration infrastructure (OLAP) and the languages used by the applications (keyword queries, SQL, etc.).

Our query model, on the other hand, is built on the assumption that integration should begin at the query or application level. The goal is to specify a query model that can express concepts from diverse interaction models in a unified and intuitive way. We focus on the applications related to the areas of databases, information retrieval, and complex networks (Fig. 3). Our model can also be used in machine learning tasks, as discussed in [16].

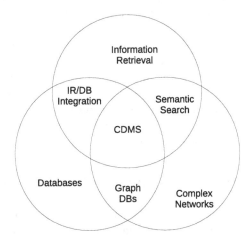

Fig. 3. CDMS in the intersection of multiple areas

The two main groups of models for data driven applications today are those associated with Information Retrieval and Database Systems. It is natural that these two areas attained such distinction over the last decades. They together cover a broad range of the data structuring spectrum – from unstructured data in documents to structured data in relations. Typical applications in IR include search engines, recommendation systems, social networks etc. Applications taking advantage of DBMSs are ubiquitous, being through traditional relational databases or the more recent models for document databases, XML and semistructured databases, graph databases and the NoSQL movement.

Complex networks, which have gained strong momentum in the last decade, is the third area completing our picture. Complex networks, whose techniques are often applied in typical IR and DB tasks, is an important area to cover in an integration framework. More importantly, we consider complex networks a fundamental piece to establish the basis of the integrated framework. To specify a query language that could be used in such a diverse scenario it is important to unify characteristics of the different interaction models.

Keyword queries and ranking are important concepts from IR, as other integration approaches have identified [2, 9, 33]. Significant research efforts have been dedicated to enable efficient ranking and keyword queries in a wider range of data models (e.g. relational, XML). In databases, declarative languages offer effective means for online interaction with data. Furthermore, the declarative approach offers opportunities for transparent query optimization. Complex networks offer a range of techniques to assess important characteristics of the data based on the underlying connections. These techniques are employed in diverse scenarios, such as the use of relevance metrics (e.g. HITS, PageRank) for IR purposes.

Here we defined a query model that embodies characteristics from all the discussed areas, providing a declarative query language that can express structured predicates, keyword queries, network topology-aware metrics, and compose results (optionally) as ranked lists. The challenge is to enable all these features over the unified graph model (LLG) presented.

Declarative querying and traditional database concepts like selections, projections and aggregations are already provided by RDF query languages such as SPARQL. The remaining issues are related to enabling IR-like ranking metrics that now have to be reinterpreted in an RDF graph setting. To enable this extended querying mechanism, we reinterpret this topology-aware metric in a common graph processing model that we call Targeted Spreading Activation (TSA), described in the following section.

5   Ranking Metrics and Language Integration

Correlating data is an important and defining characteristic for many of the applications we want to cover. To enable a high level of flexibility for correlations, we specify a set of ranking metrics which are influenced by information retrieval applications and complex networks concepts. The selection of the specific metrics aims at covering a wide range of applications while also being simple to use and understand. In the process of defining these metrics, we started with some popular metrics used in IR and then expanded the set according to the applications we wanted to cover. The set of metrics we define can be organized in the taxonomy presented in Fig. 4.

The basis of our taxonomy is the concept of comparison. Our metrics are meant to compare elements in the graph and generate a score that represents the strength of the association. The peculiar aspect about our metrics is that the scores are generated based on analysis of the topology of the graph, in contrast to most ranking approaches that are based on attributes of the elements.

There are two main groups of comparisons. Set comparisons corresponds to comparisons among elements from a finite set. Reputation and Influence are the

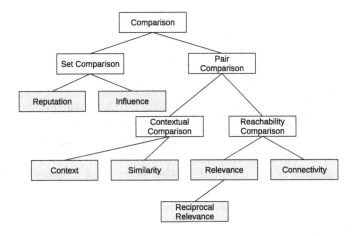

Fig. 4. Taxonomy for the adopted ranking metrics

metrics in this category. They assess, using different strategies, how well a node performs as a hub for information. The definitions of the metrics, as well as details on their interpretation, are presented in the next section.

Pair comparisons are applied to individual pairs of nodes. They assess properties of the topology surrounding or connecting the two nodes. The similarity and context metrics, classified under contextual comparison, assess the commonalities in respect to elements (nodes or relationships) surrounding the comparing nodes. Relevance and connectivity, classified under reachability comparison, assess properties of the paths interconnecting the comparing nodes.

As far as we know, this is the first time that these metrics are considered and defined under the same conceptual framework. These metrics express cognitive processes or patterns that we use to assess correlation of entities in the real world, and which are the basis of many data-driven applications, as we intend to portray along the text. We now describe our metrics and define them from a graph analysis perspective.

5.1 Graph Interpretation of the Metrics

The translation of the ranking metrics to the unified graph strategy is a challenging task. Here we adopt a Spreading Activation (SA) [12] model for our novel interpretation of the metrics.

The Targeted Spreading Activation Model: Spreading Activation (SA) processes [12] were developed to infer relationships among nodes in associative networks. The mechanism is based on traversing the network from an initial set of nodes, activating new nodes until certain stop conditions are reached. By controlling several aspects related to this activation flow, it is possible to infer and quantify the relationships of the initial nodes to the reached ones.

This simple model has the fundamental requirements for the type of correlations we want to provide for complex data:

(i) it can derive correlations among any two sets of initial nodes and destination nodes; This is important to enable modeling of several correlation metrics, as described in Sect. 5.1.

(ii) the final value of the correlations decreases as the length of the contributing paths grows; This reflects the intuitive perception that closer elements are more correlated. The model allows tuning of this characteristic through a parameter for potential degradation.

(iii) the degradation of the potential imposes boundaries to query processing;

(iv) it can be implemented as graph traversal patterns [27]; The processing of these patterns are centered in origin nodes, resulting in localized processing. The computation of these patterns requires less memory than global ranking metrics such as PageRank and HITS. This type of computation is supported by several graph database systems[3].

We tweak the basic SA model by adding mechanisms to (i) adapt the process to the labeled graph model used, (ii) consider relationship weights, (iii) add a more strict and predictable termination condition, and (iv) make the process aware of the target elements. The last point is key to the semantics of the SA process for querying complex data and also to improve optimization opportunities. We named the proposed SA variation as Targeted Spreading Activation (TSA).

The TSA model used here is defined by the parameters G, N, I, O, a, t, d, c, l, and dir described, alongside other definitions, in Table 1. A TSA process starts with origin nodes initially activated with potential a. Output potentials for each subsequent node are calculated by the function O. The output potential is spread through all relationships whose labels are in l that follow directions in dir. The potential for the reached nodes is calculated by function I. For the next iteration, the potential is spread to subsequent nodes, restarting the process, as long as the potential for reached nodes is higher than t and the number of iterations is lower than c.

Although simple in its definition, this is a very expressive model to build flexible correlation metrics. By specifying appropriate parameters and combining subsequent executions of TSAs, it is possible to define metrics that encompass concepts like relevance, reputation and similarity (Sect. 5.1). These metrics can be integrated in a declarative language with applications to a wide range of modern querying scenarios (Sect. 5.3).

Being the core of the querying process mechanism, the TSA process becomes the main target for query optimization strategies. Like with any other data or processing model, the practicability of TSA-based querying depends on architectural mechanisms to support data access optimizations and heuristics to provide approximate answers. Optimization issues were addressed in [15].

---

[3] A good overview of applications and systems can be found in http://markorodriguez. com/2013/01/09/on-graph-computing/.

Table 1. Notation used in the definitions

Notation	Description
$SA(N)$	a set of activated nodes after the execution of the spread activation process
$SA(M)_n$	value for the potential of node n after the execution of the spread activation with initial activated nodes M
a, t, d, c	respectively, initial activation potential, firing threshold, decay factor, maximum number of iterations (depth)
l	set of labels that determine valid nodes for traversal
dir	$dir \subset \{inbound, outbound\}$; set of directions for traversal
$\overline{dir}$	$dir \cap \{inbound, outbound\}$; reversed directions of dir
$\overline{SA(m)_n}$	same as $SA(m)_n$ with reversed directions, i.e. $dir \leftarrow \overline{dir}$
$I(n)$	function that calculates the input potential of a node. $I(n) = \sum_{m \in ant(n)} O(i)$ in the default case
$O(n)$	function that calculates the output potential of a node. $O(n) = I(n) * d$ in the default case
$ant(n)$	set of antecedent nodes, i.e. nodes linked to n through relationships in l that follow the directions in dir
$sub(n)$	set of subsequent nodes, i.e. nodes linked to n through relationships in l that follow the directions in $\overline{dir}$
$p(SA(N))$	set of activation paths (for each node in $SA(N)$)
$|S|$	number of elements in set S

IR Metrics According to the TSA Model: In the TSA model, to assess the rank of the relationship of nodes according to a metric, an activation potential is placed at the target elements defined in the query. The potential is spread across the topology of the graph, losing or gaining strength based on the IR metric, length of the path, or properties of the traversed elements. The metric-specific definitions of the TSA processes are presented below.

Definition 1. $relevance(m, n) = SA(\{m\})_n$,
with $O(n) = \dfrac{I(n) * d}{|sub(n)|}$

Relevance between two nodes is a measure that encompasses correlation and specificity. Correlation is proportional to the number of paths linking the two nodes and inversely proportional to the length of the paths. Specificity favors more discriminative paths (i.e. paths with fewer ramifications. It is easy to observe that this definition resembles the definition of relevance between queries and documents in a information retrieval setting. Traditional tf or idf term weighting can be readily emulated in our scheme when terms, queries and documents become nodes of a graph. Our definition is, however, a generalization of the concept that can be applied to any type of graph data and with any number or type of relationships in between m and n.

Definition 2. $rrelevance(m, n) = SA(\{m\})_n + \overline{SA(\{n\})_m}$,
with $O(n) = \dfrac{I(n) * d}{|sub(n)|}$

Reciprocal Relevance (RRelevance) between two nodes aggregates the relevance in both directions. In an information retrieval setting, it would be equivalent to aggregating tf and idf in the same metric.

Definition 3. $connectivity(m, n) = SA(\{m\})_n$

Connectivity between two nodes is a measure that assesses how interconnected two nodes are. The score is proportional to the number of paths linking the nodes in the network activated by the SA algorithm.

Definition 4. $reputation(n, N) = SA(N)_n$

Reputation of a node measures how effective it is as a hub for information flow. Here the nodes of interest are activated at the beginning and the ranking scheme favors nodes that are revisited in the sequence of the SA process. This is a simple but convenient interpretations in scenarios where the reputation cannot be pre-calculated due to high update rates, variability in the types of relationships used for the queries, or need to bias the scores based on a set of initial nodes (as in [34]).

Definition 5. $influence(n) = |(SA(\{n\}))|$

Influence is a specialization of reputation where the only concern is the number of nodes reached from the origin. The topology of the graph – in/outdegree or cycles – do not influence the metric.

Definition 6. $similarity(m, n) = \dfrac{|p(SA(\{n\})) \cap p(SA(\{m\}))|}{|p(SA(\{n\})) \cup p(SA(\{m\}))|}$

Similarity measures the ratio of common relationships (same edge label linking common nodes) between two nodes.

Definition 7. $context(m, n) = \dfrac{|SA(\{n\}) \cap SA(\{m\})|}{|SA(\{n\}) \cup SA(\{m\})|}$

Context is a specialization of similarity where edge labels do not matter.

5.2 Semantics of Ranking Metrics in Queries

Having the ranking metrics interpreted as graph analysis tasks, there is now the need of integrating these metrics in a declarative language. As opposed to creating an entirely new query language, we decided to leverage existing languages by defining an extension language that can be integrated into other languages. To that extent, we first define the semantics of the intended integration.

In our model, the proposed ranking metrics are intended to be used with graph query languages that offer: (i) means to reference individual nodes in the graph, (ii) selection of match variables, and (iii) query results as a set of tuples (or a graph representation of). These are basic components of graph languages like SPARQL and Cypher. A ranking metric can refer to:

- a single match variable (set of vertices), e.g. "rank papers from EDBT 2013 according to <u>first author</u> *reputation*", where first author is the match variable in question (e.g. "SELECT ?firstAuthor ..." in SPARQL);
- a given vertex[4] and a match variable, e.g. "rank papers according to *relevance* of their <u>first author</u> (match variable) to the topic <u>data integration</u> (vertex)";
- two match variables, e.g. "rank papers according to *relevance* of the <u>first author</u> to the topic in the <u>first keyword of the paper</u>".

Conceptually, the ranking metrics are applied to query results, generating a ranking value for each returned tuple. In practice, to speed up query processing, results would be approximate and the rank would be generated for some of the nodes based on access pattern heuristics.

5.3   Extending Declarative Queries

Having the ranking metrics interpreted as graph analysis tasks, it is possible to integrate them in a declarative query language. As opposed to creating an entirely new query language, we decided to leverage existing languages by defining an extension language.

A convenient way to integrate the ranking metrics into existing query languages is to add a "RANK BY" clause. The clause should enable an arbitrary combination of metrics that expresses the global ranking condition defined by the user. We encode the clause in the extension query language that we denominated in* (or in star). in* can be used to extend other languages, for example, extended SPARQL becomes inSPARQL by convention. More details about the language and its design principles can be found in [17].

```
 1 ExtendedQuery::=RegularQuery RankClause
 2 RankClause::='RANK BY' RankMetric ( ',' RankMetric )*
 3 RankMetric::= Weight? ( UnaryRMetricDesc | BinaryRMetricDesc )
 4 UnaryRMetricDesc::=UnaryRankMetric 'OF' MatchVariable
 5         Modifiers*
 6 BinaryRMetricDesc::=BinaryRankMetric 'OF' MatchVariable 'TO'
 7         ( MatchVariable | Vertex | KWQuery) Modifiers*
 8 UnaryRankMetric::=Reputation | Influence
 9 BinaryRankMetric::=Relevance | Connectivity | Similarity | Context
10Modifiers::=Follow | Depth | Direction | Weighted
11Follow::='FOLLOW' EdgeSet
12Depth::='DEPTH' INTEGER
13Direction:=='DIRECTION' ( 'INBOUND' | 'OUTBOUND' | 'BOTH' )
14Weighted:=='WEIGHTED'
15KWQuery:=='KWQUERY' '(' String ')'
16EdgeSet:=='(' Edge ( ',' Edge )* ')' . . .
```

Fig. 5. Simplified BNF grammar for the proposed extension (terminators omitted)

---

[4] as defined previously, a keyword query would also be a node in the graph.

Note that the extension causes query semantics and result interpretation to change, therefore, any extended language would be more adequately described as new language based on the syntax of the original language. This suggests an incidental meaning for an acronym like inSPARQL: recursively, "inSPARQL is Not SPARQL".

Figure 5 shows a simplified BNF grammar of the proposed extension. A ranking can be specified as mix of weighted ranking metrics (lines 2 and 3). Weights capture the relative importance of each metric. The scores generated by the metrics are normalized before the calculation of the final weighted score.

Ranking metrics are unary or binary. Unary ranking metrics are applied to a single match variable (lines 4 and 5). Binary ranking metrics can be applied to a match variable and a named vertex or between two match variables.

The language allows for modifiers (lines 10 to 14) to be applied to the ranking definitions. These modifiers define the parameters for the execution of the SA algorithm. FOLLOW specifies valid edges for the algorithm to traverse. DEPTH defines the maximum length for the traversal paths. DIRECTION sets the direction of traversal as outbound, inbound or both (default) edges. WEIGHTED makes edge weights influence the degradation of the activation potential (the potential is multiplied by the weight).

The combination of the IR-inspired metrics in a declarative querying setting enables a high level of flexibility and expressiveness for the applications to explore. In the next section we show and discuss some examples of queries that can be used for practical applications.

5.4   Applications

This section presents examples of queries in the extended SPARQL language. These queries are meant to demonstrate the expressiveness of the approach in a wide range of applications.

Search engines/CMSs: Figure 6a shows a possible implementation for a document retrieval query using topic modeling. The keyword query is expressed by the function KWQUERY[5] and the relevance is assessed as if the query was a node in the graph. The query also takes into account the reputation of the authors and the relevance of documents to the topic :Politics (assessed based on the connections between the query node and documents that are created by a Topic Modeling algorithm such as LDA). Data management aspects discussed in the next section would be interesting matches to implement novel CMS architectures like in Ngomo et al. [26]. Our metrics would also allow query answering based on the context of the user or a context defined by the user, implementing a query model such as the one proposed by [28]. Graph-based term weighting [7] could also be simulated in our query model.

Recommendation systems: Figure 6b shows a product recommendation query that finds products that the client Bob (with uri :bob) has not purchased.

---

[5] KWQUERY is a syntactical shortcut that represents an underlying mapper as in Sect. 6.1.

The query traverses Bob's friendship network to find products purchased by his friends that might be relevant to him. The spreading activation interpretation of this query evaluation also implies that products purchased by Bob, even though they do not appear in the results, will be traversed on the way to customers that have co-purchased these products, which in turn will activate other products from these customers.

Social Networks: Figure 6c shows a query that could be used for friend suggestion on a social network application. It ranks the top 5 persons over a given age based on the similarity of hobbies and movie preferences of user Alice.

Collaborative filtering: Figure 6d shows a query that filters posts from pages that friends of user Carol follow. The posts are ranked based on their influence in the network.

Decision support: Figure 6e shows a query that can be used to prospect for employees that would be good candidates to replace a manager (Charlie) in his post. The query favors employees strongly related to a (presumably important)

(a)
```
SELECT ?doc, ?author
 WHERE { ?doc :type :BlogPost }
RANK BY (2 KW, 1 PoliticsTopic, 3 AuthorRep)
 2 RELEVANCE OF ?doc TO KWQUERY(``US elections'')
 1 RELEVANCE OF ?doc TO :Politics
 3 REPUTATION OF ?author
```

(b)
```
SELECT DISTINCT ?product
 WHERE { ?product :type :Product .
   FILTER NOT EXISTS (:bob :purchased ?product)}
RANK BY RELEVANCE OF ?product TO :bob
 FOLLOW (:friendsWith, :purchased)
 DEPTH 3 DIRECTION BOTH
```

(c)
```
SELECT ?person
 WHERE { ?person :hasAge ?age .
     FILTER (?age > 30)}
LIMIT 5
RANK BY SIMILARITY OF ?person TO :alice
 FOLLOW (:hasHobby, :favoriteMovie)
```

(d)
```
SELECT ?post, ?page
 WHERE { :carol :closeFriend ?closeFriend .
     ?closeFriend :follows ?page .
     ?page :publishes ?post .
     ?post :date ?date .
     FILTER(?date = "2012-12-12"^^xsd:date)}
RANK BY INFLUENCE OF ?post
```

(e)
```
SELECT ?employee
 WHERE { ?employee :worksFor :research}
RANK BY
 2 RELEVANCE OF ?employee TO :yPhone
 1 CONTEXT OF ?employee TO :Charlie
```

Fig. 6. Examples of extended SPARQL queries (namespaces have been omitted)

product (yPhone) and also those that have professional contexts similar to the current manager.

Other applications: Similar queries could be used in several other scenarios, especially the ones with richly interconnected data and that require complex analysis of the correlations. Some examples are Semantic Web inference applications, were assessing correlations between classes and candidate instances can be complex [1]. The scientific domain is another interesting application field. For example, in a database with food network relationships, a query could identify relevant species or areas for conservation efforts.

6   Relationship Management in the CDMS

We have so far discussed our data and query models, with little focus on implementation or architectural aspects. The proposed query model implies new requirements for user interaction, query processing and data management. The CDMS is responsible for encompassing all these aspects in a coherent architecture.

The querying mechanism presented so far is based on the observation that relationship analysis is central to several applications and the basis for evaluating the metrics introduced here. Besides providing a query language that enables expressive correlation clauses, it is important to provide the CDMS with mechanisms to manage diverse aspects of relationship life cycle. Here we show how such mechanisms could provide better support for data integration tasks and increase the expressiveness of the query language.

6.1   Mappers

Relationship creation is an important and defining operation for the described application scenarios. For example, several text indexing tasks, such as topic modeling, derive relationships between the text and more general concepts. To support these types of task, an integrated framework must provide mechanisms to facilitate the creation of these relationships in the unified graph. The same type of mapping between source data and the unified graph is required for other types of data such as relational or semi-structured.

In our framework, the creation of relationships is encapsulated in *MAP* statements. Figure 7 shows an example (detailed in the experiments section) of such DML (Data Manipulation Language) query. The MAP statement (that triggers a *mapper*) is also encoded as an extension of a graph query language (SPARQL, in this case). The query selects all nodes of type 'film' and their respective labels. The selected elements are used to call the mapper *TokenMapper*.

Mappers are very similar to *stored procedures*. What sets them apart are (i) their integrated use in our ranking queries, and (ii) how they are hooked in the databases's API so that any new data that matches the mapping criterion is passed through appropriate mappers. Point (ii) is not yet supported by our framework. (i) is discussed in the experiment section.

```
MAP DISTINCT ?movie, ?label
WITH TokenMapper
WHERE{
    ?movie a movie:film .
    ?movie rdfs:label ?label }
```

Fig. 7. MAP statement applying mapper *TokenMapper* to movies and their labels

Mappers are the mechanism that underlie the creation of the LLG. In a wider perspective, mappings are however not restricted to model transformations, but also allow transformations of data already in the unified graph, for example, to infer new relationships based on correlations between nodes. These ad hoc mappings are especially important for querying and analyzing data, enabling users to manipulate the underlying data at query time without the obligation to materialize the new relationships. For this reason, our approach addresses query and mapping as an interdependent and symbiotic process of data analysis and exploration.

A mapping process stores metadata related to the creation of the relationships, which can be explored at query time. Since relationships are associated with their mappers, multiple mappers can be used for the same type of relationship. For example, multiple text indexing strategies can be used simultaneously, then queries can specify the strategy that best fits the information need or simply take advantage of the multiple connections created by the diverse mappers.

Metadata about creation time and usage statistics of the relationships can also be used in a more expressive version of the extended query language presented here. Query modifiers could refer to this metadata to favor *novelty* or *popularity* (also important concepts in IR) of the relationships.

7 Experiments

We now show experiments that aim at demonstrating what we envision as a typical usage scenario for our framework. The database used in the experiments is the Linked Movie Data Base (LinkedMDB) [19], which we think is a good representative for the type of unified graph we aim at. The database integrates data from several sources (FreeBase, OMDB, DBpedia, Geonames, etc.). The process used to semantically integrate the distinct sources is similar to what is done in a typical Data Warehouse and precisely what we envision to be the workflow for the usage scenarios of our framework (i.e. integration of institutional data). The database contains 3,579,616 triples. The dataset has other important characteristics: (i) it encompasses the bulk of the production in an important area of human activity, (ii) data elements have clear semantics, (iii) data elements are organized based on several characteristics (type, genre, subject, etc.) and correlated in a complex graph topology. These characteristics support the applicability of our framework in real scenarios.

We implemented a basic mapper (TokenMapper) that maps input nodes into tokens present in their labels. The tokens are themselves stored as nodes in the

```
PREFIX movie: <http://data.linkedmdb.org/resource/movie/>
PREFIX skos: <http://www.w3.org/2004/02/skos/core#>
PREFIX foaf: <http://xmlns.com/foaf/0.1/>
SELECT DISTINCT ?movie where{
  ?movie a movie:film .
  ?movie movie:initial_release_date ?date .
  FILTER ( fn:substring(?date, 1, 4) > "1990" ) .
  FILTER EXISTS { ?movie foaf:page ?page }
}
RANKED BY
  2 RELEVANCE OF ?movie TO
    TokenMapper("My favorite films are Matrix and Avatar")
    DEPTH 2 FOLLOW TokenMapper:hasToken,
  1 RELEVANCE OF ?movie TO movie:film_subject/461
    DEPTH 5 FOLLOW skos:subject
```

Fig. 8. Query that ranks movies according to relevance to a preferences text and to the subject "Virtual Reality" (film_subject/461)

graph database. The mapper receives as arguments the source node for the mappings and the text content to be mapped. This mapping uses a standard query analyzer (from Lucene's library) that simply lowercases, removes stop words, and tokenizes the text. We are using this strategy for its simplicity and didacticism. In a real scenario, more modern techniques such as NER (Named Entity Recognition), LSA (Latent Semantic Analysis) or ESA (Explicit Semantics Analysis) would provide more efficient and meaningful mappings.

Table 2. Top-15 ranked results for the first query

top 15	name
0.67	Avatar
0.67	Avatar
0.55	The Matrix
0.53	The Matrix Revolutions
0.53	The Matrix Reloaded
0.33	The Thirteenth Floor
0.33	EXistenZ
0.33	Lawnmower Man 2: Beyond Cyberspace
0.33	Storm Watch (aka Code Hunter)
0.33	Strange Days
0.33	The Lawnmower Man
0.33	Welcome to Blood City
0.21	The Favorite
0.19	The Matrix Online
0.19	The Matrix Revisited

The DML query used for our mapping is shown in Fig. 7. We are mapping the label of movies to tokens. Executing the query triggers the mapping of each selected movie, generating the appropriate nodes for the tokens when needed. This same mapper can be used in the ranking clause, as will be shown below.

We now present analysis of queries to demonstrate the use of the metrics and mappers. At this point of development of our framework, we are focusing on the relevance and connectivity metrics, which we regard as having widespread applications and presenting the biggest challenges for query processing.

The first query (Fig. 8) retrieves and ranks movies relevant to a text stating movie preferences and that are also relevant to the subject 'Virtual Reality'. This type of query can be derived from user's profiles, for example. The query also selects elements based on structured predicates, specifying that returned movies should have a home page relationship and have been released after 1990.

The evaluation of this query can be divided in two phases: (i) graph matching and structured selection, and (ii) ranking based on topological properties. This separation in two distinct phases is only conceptual however. A query processor is free to combine the phases in any fashion to optimize the evaluation.

In the graph matching and selection phase, the triple pattern is matched against the data graph, the results are filtered according to the structured predicates. In the second phase, the multiple ranking criteria are evaluated.

The first ranking criterion is relevance to the text. To assess the scores for this metric, the query processor creates a temporary node and appropriate mappings are made using the specified mapper (TokenMapper). The spreading activation process is then executed to assess the correlation between each movie and the temporary node. The process is set to follow the relationships created by the mapper (hasToken). This is a typical mechanism for a keyword query type of interaction in our framework. A system-wide default keyword query mapper can be set so that queries can use the reserved KWQuery element, so that the parser automatically assigns the appropriate mapper and relationships to follow (as in Fig. 6a).

The second ranking criterion assesses correlation between movies and the subject "Virtual Reality". The resulting scores from each criterion are normalized and aggregated, according to the specified weights, to generate the final score. The results (Table 2) show contributions from both ranking criteria. The movie Avatar is not directly related to the subject "Virtual Reality", owing its high ranking to the high tf*idf value of its name (note that tf*idfs are not calculated, this is an emergent property of the relevance metric which is not restricted to text-based rankings)[6]. All movies from the Matrix franchise have scores combining both criteria. Lower ranking results also provide insight into the interplay between the rankings for this query (e.g. 'The Favorite' matches the keyword query with a lower tf*idf-like score).

The second query (Fig. 9) uses the connectivity metric to discover films correlated to 'The Silence of the Lambs'. The query specifies that the analysis

---

[6] The second Avatar record refers to a lesser known Singaporean film (introducing a *reputation* metric in the query would certainly lower its score).

```
PREFIX film: <http://data.linkedmdb.org/resource/film/>
PREFIX resource: <http://data.linkedmdb.org/resource/movie/>
PREFIX skos: <http://www.w3.org/2004/02/skos/core#>
SELECT DISTINCT ?movie WHERE{
  ?movie a resource:film .
  ?movie resource:initial_release_date ?date .
  FILTER ( fn:starts-with(?date, "199")
}
RANKED BY
  CONNECTIVITY OF ?movie TO film:38145
  DEPTH 4 FOLLOW (skos:subject, resource:director)
```

Fig. 9. Query that retrieves films correlated to 'The Silence of the Lambs' (film:38145)

Table 3. Top-10 ranked results for the second query

top 10	name
1.0	The Silence of the Lambs
0.81	Man Bites Dog
0.80	Natural Born Killers
0.80	Butterfly Kiss
0.80	Freeway
0.79	Seven
0.79	Aileen Wuornos: The Selling of a Serial Killer
0.79	Serial Mom
0.79	Copycat
0.79	The Young Poisoner's Handbook

Table 4. Top-10 ranked results for the first query

top 10	name
1.0	The Silence of the Lambs
0.34	Philadelphia
0.34	Cousin Bobby
0.25	Man Bites Dog
0.25	Natural Born Killers
0.25	Butterfly Kiss
0.24	Freeway
0.23	Seven
0.23	Aileen Wuornos: The Selling of a Serial Killer
0.23	Serial Mom

should consider only the relationships 'movie:director' and 'skos:subject'. It is interesting to note that setting the modifier *depth* to 4 means that indirect correlations are also considered. For example, a film could receive a positive score even though it does not share a subject with 'The Silence of the Lambs', as long as it is correlated with a film that does share a subject.

The results for the query are shown in Table 3. The output is strongly biased towards scores generated by correlations through common subjects (which tend to form tighter clusters). If the user wants to increase the importance of the 'director' relationship to retrieve more movies correlated to the director of 'The Silence of the Lambs', the user can separate the relationships into two ranking criteria. This type of user interactivity is another important advantage our declarative querying scheme. The results of splitting the rankings in such a way are presented in Table 4. The results are for a version of the query that used a 3:1 weight division favoring the *director* relationship.

8   Related Work

We now discuss related work on data integration in various levels: from data access integration, through syntactic/semantic integration, and up to application or query model integration. Integration at any level is highly dependent on the lower levels.

8.1   Data Access Integration

The first level of integration must provide a unique access point for the data. This can be accomplished by basically two approaches: centralizing the data or connecting the data sources in an infrastructure that simulates a centralized repository. Centralized integration of institutional data is typically related to the deployment of data warehouses or data marts [21]. Data centralization approaches have also been proposed in the context of the Semantic Web [19], and the DBpedia project[7] is a notable example of this type of approach.

The research on Federated Databases aims at providing a unified view of the data while maintaining the autonomy of the data sources [32]. In the context of the Semantic Web, Schwarte et al. [31] have proposed a federation layer for Linked Open Data. Schenk and Staab [30] have proposed a mechanism for the specification of views over Linked Data, enabling declarative federation of data sources.

Our framework is independent of the specific strategy chosen for data access integration. The requirement is that all interaction is done as if the data was integrated in a unified graph. Whether this integration is done through federation or physically integrating the data is an architectural decision based on expectations of performance and requirements for preserving the autonomy of data sources.

---

[7] http://dbpedia.org/.

8.2   Data Model Integration

Data integration requires enabling data manipulation under a unified model. Federated databases frequently employ the relational model (common among data sources) for the integration. Data minig, which has application-specific requirements, favors the multidimensional model [22].

In the Semantic Web, the adopted unifying model is the RDF graph. The Resource Description Framework (RDF)[8] is a general-purpose language created for representing information about resources in the Web. The basic unit of information is a statement triple, which contains a subject, a predicate, and an object. All elements in a triple are identified by URIs (except for objects that can also be literal values). Triples can refer to each other, forming a graph. The advantage of the RDF model comes from its simplicity, enabling the representation of data from a wide range of domains.

There has been a substantial amount of research in mapping other data models into RDF [3,6]. The W3C RDB2RDF Working Group[9] is defining languages and standards for mapping relational databases into RDF.

Besides having the data in a unified representation model, it is important to correlate data from the diverse sources into unified concepts. In the relational world, this process is know as record deduplication or linkage and is part of the ETL (Extraction Transformation Loading) workflow [18]. In the Semantic Web, the usual way to represent these correlations is the creation of *sameAs* relationships between entities. These relationships can be created manually or by automated processes. Hassanzadeh and Consens [19] employ several string matching techniques to correlate Linked Open Data from diverse sources to create an interlinked version of a movies database.

In this proposal, we assume that the institutional data is integrated in an RDF graph. This allows us to take advantage of other standardized technologies developed in the context of the WWW and the Semantic Web, such as universal identification through URIs, semantic integration through *sameAs* relationships, and the SPARQL query language.

8.3   Query Model Integration

Once data is integrated, it becomes possible to pose queries that could not be answered before, producing more valuable information for institutions and the public. The integration approaches, however, typically focus on integrating data under a specific query model, such as the relational or OLAP. This usually constrains the range of data models that can be integrate and, foremost, restricts direct querying of the integrated data from applications that use other query models.

Recently, there has been initiatives aimed at tackling integration at the application/query level. The research community has identified the interplay between

---

[8] http://www.w3.org/RDF/.

[9] http://www.w3.org/2001/sw/rdb2rdf/.

the fields of Databases (DB) and Information Retrieval (IR) as a means to improve data integration and query expressiveness across applications [2, 9]. The drive to integrate the areas stems from the fact that they represent the bulk of data stored and processed across institutions. Furthermore, either field has been very successful by their own but still faces challenges when dealing with interactions typical to the other field.

The integration of the IR and DB areas has been an important topic in the agenda of the research community for many years. Following the initial identification of challenges and applications, several successful approaches were proposed and implemented [33]. Most prominent research focuses on keyword queries over structured data and documents, top-k ranking strategies and extraction of structured information from documents.

Keyword query research draws from the simple yet effective keyword query model to allow integrated querying over documents and structured data. Most of the frameworks match keywords to documents, schema and data integrated in a graph structure. The connected matches form trees that are ranked based on variations of IR metrics such as tf*idf and PageRank. Some of the research focus on optimizing the top-k query processing [23] while others implement more effective variations of the ranking metrics [24].

Keyword queries over structured data are intended for tasks where the schema is unknown to the user. The techniques are effective for data exploration, but there is no support for more principled interactions. There are conceptual and structural mismatches among queries, data and results that make returned matches hard to predict and interpret. Furthermore, the queries can only express relevance between the provided keywords and database elements. Our query model can represent many more correlation criteria that can be combined arbitrarily in user-defined expressions. More importantly, the queries can correlated any type of data in the graph database.

The research on Top-k queries focus on enabling efficient processing of ranked queries on structured and semi-structured data. Ranking is based on scores derived from multiple predicates specified in the query. The main challenge is to compute results avoiding full computation of the expensive joins. The proposals vary on adopted query model, data access methods, implementation strategy, and assumptions on data and scoring functions (see [20] for a contextualized survey).

Scoring functions enable ranking based on properties of data elements. There is, however, no simple means to rank results based on the context of elements or how they are correlated, typical requirements for IR-like applications and a defining characteristic of our SA-based ranking scheme.

This type of contextual ranking could only be implemented in an ad-hoc fashion through complex scoring functions. Since the query processor would be unaware of the semantics of the queries and the topology of the relationships, there would be no opportunity for the optimizer to make sensible execution plans. Furthermore, the relational model assumed in most research has no means to reference individual data elements, an important requirement for effective data correlation. Our focus is on offering predicates that allows ranking based on contextual metrics not readily available as attributes. The proposal described here is complementary to regular top-k querying. It is important to support both types of ranking, since they are recurrent to many applications.

Information Extraction refers to the automatic extraction from unstructured sources of structured information such as entities, relationships between entities, and attributes describing entities [29]. Information Extraction systems employ two main techniques to harvest relationships (or facts) from text: extrapolating extraction pattens based on example seeds [13] and employing linguistic patterns to discover as many types of relationships as possible, task known as Open Information Extraction [4]. Loading the extracted facts on a DBMS allows declarative querying over the data. This is a one-way, data-centric type of integration of DB and IR. The integration proposed here focuses on unified querying and data models. The framework proposed allows easy integration of Information Extraction system's output, maximizing the benefits of both approaches.

We argue that the mentioned approaches tend to focus on infrastructure issues related to extremes of enabling the type interaction present in one area over the data model of the other. In this paper we take a top-down approach to modeling the integration, questioning what are the main and defining properties of each area, and how to offer a unified, non-modal interaction over data and query models.

9   Conclusion

We showed how modern standards and technologies developed to solve integration issues on the Web can be applied in a unifying framework for institutional data. Representing the integrated data as a graph is a good strategy for data model integration. Our main contribution is on extending this type of integration to a higher level of abstraction, tackling integration of query models.

In our approach, the key to achieve more expressiveness at the query level is the combination of flexible metrics in a declarative model. Our query model redefines several metrics that rank entities based on the topology of their correlations. To the best of our knowledge, this is the first time the metrics presented are considered and formalized under the same model. Similarly, we are not aware of other ranking strategies that enable the level of expressiveness offered by the combination of our metrics and a declarative language. This combination allows data correlation queries that cover a wide range of applications. The introduced mappers play an important role as a data management mechanism to support this high level of integration.

As suggested by the query examples presented (Fig. 6), it is possible to represent information needs that would require a level of data analysis that is beyond current implementations of typical DB or IR systems. In fact, answering the type of queries introduced here in a typical technological environment nowadays would require substantial engineering for the implementation of *ad-hoc* solutions. The expressiveness of the queries allowed by the extended languages sometimes blurs the line between declarative queries and data analysis. Given the computational requirements of such settings, it is important to introduce optimization mechanisms and heuristics to compute approximate answers. Our declarative querying scenario opens many opportunities for query optimization. Details about the mechanisms we are currently adopting are described in [15].

We expect query-level integration to become increasingly important as our technological landscape continues to diversify. We showed how our model can cover a broad range of models and applications. Our experiments indicate the practicability of our approach, especially regarding the use of mappers to simplify data integration and enable more expressive querying.

Acknowledgments. The authors would like to thank Prof. Frank Wm. Tompa for feedback and encouragement in earlier stages of this work. This work was partially financed by the Microsoft Research FAPESP Virtual Institute (NavScales project), CNPq (MuZOO Project and PRONEX-FAPESP), INCT in Web Science (CNPq 557.128/2009-9) and CAPES, with individual grants from CAPES and FAPESP (process 2012/15988-9).

References

1. Alves, H., Santanchè, A.: Abstract framework for social ontologies and folksonomized ontologies. In: SWIM. ACM (2012)
2. Amer-Yahia, S., Case, P., Rölleke, T., Shanmugasundaram, J., Weikum, G.: Report on the DB/IR panel. SIGMOD Record **34**(4), 71–74 (2005)
3. Auer, S., Dietzold, S., Lehmann, J., Hellmann, S., Aumueller, D.: Triplify: lightweight linked data publication from relational databases. In: Proceedings of the 18th International Conference on World Wide Web, WWW 2009 (2009)
4. Banko, M., Cafarella, M.J., Soderland, S., Broadhead, M., Etzioni, O.: Open information extraction from the web. In: IJCAI, pp. 2670–2676 (2007)
5. Berners-Lee, T.: Giant global graph. Online posting, 2007. http://dig.csail.mit.edu/breadcrumbs/node/215
6. Bizer, C.: D2rq - treating non-rdf databases as virtual rdf graphs. In: Proceedings of the 3rd International Semantic Web Conference (ISWC2004) (2004)
7. Blanco, R., Lioma, C.: Graph-based term weighting for information retrieval. Inf. Retr. **15**(1), 54–92 (2012)
8. Blei, D.M., Ng, A.Y., Jordan, M.I.: Latent dirichlet allocation. J. Mach. Learn. Res. **3**(4–5), 993–1022 (2003)
9. Chaudhuri, S., Ramakrishnan, R., Weikum, G.: Integrating DB and IR technologies: what is the sound of one hand clapping? In: CIDR, pp. 1–12 (2005)
10. Costa, L., Oliveira Jr., O., Travieso, G., Rodrigues, F., Boas, P., Antiqueira, L., Viana, M., Rocha, L.: Analyzing and modeling real-world phenomena with complex networks: a survey of applications. Adv. Phys. **60**, 329–412 (2011)
11. Costa, L.D.F., Rodrigues, F.A., Travieso, G., Boas, P.R.V.: Characterization of complex networks: a survey of measurements. Adv. Phys. **56**(1), 167–242 (2007)
12. Crestani, F.: Application of spreading activation techniques in information retrieval. Artif. Intell. Rev. **11**(6), 453–482 (1997)
13. Etzioni, O., Cafarella, M., Downey, D., Kok, S., Popescu, A.-M., Shaked, T., Soderland, S., Weld, D.S., Yates, A.: Web-scale information extraction in KnowItAll. In: WWW, pp. 100, 26 March 2004
14. Getoor, L., Diehl, C.P.: Link mining: a survey. SIGKDD Explor. Newsl. **7**(2), 3–12 (2005)

15. Gomes Jr., L., Costa, L., Santanchè, A.: Querying complex data. Technical Report IC-13-27, Institute of Computing, University of Campinas, October 2013
16. Gomes Jr., L., Jensen, R., Santanchè, A.: Query-based inferences in the Complex Data Management System. In: Structured Learning: Inferring Graphs from Structured and Unstructured Inputs (SLG-ICML) (2013)
17. Gomes Jr., L., Jensen, R., Santanchè, A.: Towards query model integration: topology-aware, ir-inspired metrics for declarative graph querying. In: Graph Q-EDBT (2013)
18. Han, J., Kamber, M.: Data Mining: Concepts and Techniques. Morgan Kaufmann, San Francisco (2006)
19. Hassanzadeh, O., Consens, M.: Linked movie data base. In: Proceedings of the 2nd Workshop on Linked Data on the Web (LDOW2009) (2009)
20. Ilyas, I.F., Beskales, G., Soliman, M.A.: A survey of top-k query processing techniques in relational database systems. ACM Comput. Surveys **40**(4), 11:1–11:58 (2008)
21. Imhoff, C., Galemmo, N., Geiger, J.G.: Mastering Data Warehouse Design: Relational and Dimensional Techniques. Wiley, Chichester (2003)
22. Jarke, M., Lenzerini, M., Vassiliou, Y., Vassiliadis, P.: Fundamentals of Data Warehouses. Springer, Heidelberg (2003)
23. Kimelfeld, B., Sagiv, Y.: Finding and approximating top-k answers in keyword proximity search. In: PODS (2006)
24. Luo, Y., Wang, W., Lin, X., Zhou, X., Wang, J., Li, K.: SPARK2: Top-k keyword query in relational databases. TKDE **23**(12), 1763–1780 (2011)
25. Markovitch, S., Gabrilovich, E.: Computing semantic relatedness using wikipedia-based explicit semantic analysis. In: IJCAI (2007)
26. Ngonga Ngomo, A.-C., Heino, N., Lyko, K., Speck, R., Kaltenböck, M.: SCMS – Semantifying content management systems. In: Aroyo, L., Welty, C., Alani, H., Taylor, J., Bernstein, A., Kagal, L., Noy, N., Blomqvist, E. (eds.) ISWC 2011, Part II. LNCS, vol. 7032, pp. 189–204. Springer, Heidelberg (2011)
27. Rodriguez, M.A., Neubauer, P.: The graph traversal pattern. CoRR, abs/1004.1001 (2010)
28. Rodriguez, M.A., Pepe, A., Shinavier, J.: The dilated triple. In: Badr, Y., Chbeir, R., Abraham, A., Hassanien, A.-E. (eds.) Emergent Web Intelligence: Advanced Semantic Technologies, pp. 3–16. Springer, London (2010)
29. Sarawagi, S.: Information extraction. Found. Trends Databases **1**(3), 261–377 (2008)
30. Schenk, S., Staab, S.: newblock Networked graphs: a declarative mechanism for SPARQL rules, SPARQL views and RDF data integration on the web. In: WWW (2008)
31. Schwarte, A., Haase, P., Hose, K., Schenkel, R., Schmidt, M.: FedX: A federation layer for distributed query processing on linked open data. In: Antoniou, G., Grobelnik, M., Simperl, E., Parsia, B., Plexousakis, D., De Leenheer, P., Pan, J. (eds.) ESWC 2011, Part II. LNCS, vol. 6644, pp. 481–486. Springer, Heidelberg (2011)
32. Sheth, A., Larson, J.: Federated database systems for managing distributed, heterogeneous, and autonomous databases. ACM Comput. Surveys **22**(3), 183–236 (1990)
33. Weikum, G., Kasneci, G., Ramanath, M., Suchanek, F.: Database and information-retrieval methods for knowledge discovery. Commun. ACM **52**(4), 56–64 (2009)
34. White, S. Smyth, P.: Algorithms for estimating relative importance in networks. In: SIGKDD (2003)

Dimensional Clustering of Linked Data: Techniques and Applications

Alfio Ferrara, Lorenzo Genta, Stefano Montanelli$^{(\boxtimes)}$, and Silvana Castano

Università degli Studi di Milano,
DI -Via Comelico, 39, 20135 Milano, Italy
{alfio.ferrara,lorenzo.genta,stefano.montanelli,silvana.castano}@unimi.it

Abstract. The plurality and heterogeneity of linked data features require appropriate solutions for accurate matching and clustering. In this paper, we propose a dimensional clustering approach to enforce (i) the capability to select the set of features to use for data matching and clustering, that are packaged into the so-called *thematic dimension*, and (ii) the capability to make explicit the *cause of similarity* that generates each cluster. Ensemble techniques for combining different single-dimension cluster sets into a sort of multi-dimensional view of the considered linked data are also presented as a further contribution of the paper. Application to linked data summarization and exploration is finally discussed.

1 Introduction

The main consequence of the adoption of the linked data principles by some of the main providers of open and structured data on the web, such as DBpedia and Freebase, is the availability of large collections of data that can be accessed through public services and search endpoints [4]. Linked data are usually designed for answering to a general-purpose informative need and they are characterized by a large number of features. Some of these features are related to the internal structure of the linked data repository at hand (e.g., the name of the user who inserted a data resource) and they are mostly useless for satisfying user queries about specific interests. Some other features are intended to provide an informative description of the real object represented by the linked data resource (e.g., person names, locations, professions) and they are usually very numerous and heterogeneous in kind. This plurality and heterogeneity of features need to be properly considered for accurate matching and clustering processes [12,24]. State-of-the-art approaches for linked data clustering aggregate in the same cluster semantically-related linked data resources based on similarity metrics proportional to the number of common features between them [6,9]. However, with a conventional clustering approach, all the features indifferently concur to determine the similarity value of different linked data resources and this is a limitation for an effective exploitation of resulting linked data clusters. In fact, considering all the features together in a flat way produces a "monolithic" classification, where clusters are generally characterized by quite-low similarity values where many pairs of resources with the same degree of similarity converge in the same

© Springer-Verlag Berlin Heidelberg 2015
A. Hameurlain et al. (Eds.): TLDKS XIX, LNCS 8990, pp. 55–86, 2015.
DOI: 10.1007/978-3-662-46562-2_3

cluster, but not necessarily originated by the same features. This way, it is also difficult to mine the causes of similarity that generate a given cluster, making the meaning understanding of the resulting cluster sometimes not very immediate and easy.

In this paper, we overcome the above limitations of conventional linked data clustering by proposing a dimensional clustering approach to create similarity-based views of linked data by enforcing (i) the capability to select the set of features to use for data matching and clustering, that are packaged into the so-called *thematic dimension*, and (ii) the capability to make explicit the *cause of similarity* that generates each cluster. As a result, different dimensional cluster sets are produced, each one focused on a given thematic dimension. Resources with the same degree of similarity but different set of matching features are put in different clusters, resulting in a more accurate and focused classification result. Moreover, we define ensemble techniques to enforce the combination of different single-dimension cluster sets into multi-dimension cluster sets, to provide a sort of multi-dimensional view of a given set of linked data. Providing advanced information retrieval and exploration services is strongly related to the capability of reducing the data complexity by providing high-level, summary views of semantically-related data. To this end, in the paper, we describe the application of the proposed dimensional clustering techniques to support linked data summarization and exploration.

The paper is organized as follows. In Sect. 2, we present the motivating example of our work. The proposed approach to dimensional data clustering is illustrated in Sect. 3. Matching and clustering techniques for dimensional data clustering are discussed in Sects. 4 and 5, respectively. Techniques for cluster ensemble are presented in Sect. 6. In Sect. 7, we envisage the application of dimensional clustering to linked data exploration. In Sect. 8, we illustrate the results of our experimental evaluation. Related work and concluding remarks are finally provided in Sects. 9 and 10, respectively.

2   Motivating Example

Consider a corpus of linked data about a certain topic of interest, such as for example famous scientists in the field of computer science. A user can be interested in exploring the corpus by viewing these scientists grouped according to a specific perspective, like for example their professional qualifications (e.g., the educational background, the awards they received). In such case, the user expectation is that groups include scientists based on their similarity over those properties that describe the professional profile. The user can be also interested in exploring the same corpus of linked data by viewing scientists grouped according to another perspective, like for example the geographical one. In this case, the user expectation is to view groups containing scientists with similar values over properties like nationality, residence, and place of birth.

The dimensional clustering techniques we propose enforce the notion of **thematic dimension**. A thematic dimension is a set of linked data properties/features

$\mathcal{D}$ that are selected to express the perspective over the data to use for aggregation. A dimension is thematic in the sense that a cluster contains similar resources according to the properties/features of $\mathcal{D}$ and it represents a particular "theme" in the context of the considered dimension. In the above example about scientists in computer science, $\mathcal{D}_{pro}$ = {field, almaMater, award, doctoralAdvisor, influencedBy, influenced} and $\mathcal{D}_{geo}$ = {nationality, residence, birthPlace, deathPlace} are examples of professional and geographical thematic dimensions, respectively. A cluster containing scientists that studied in the same university is an example of theme for the professional dimension $\mathcal{D}_{pro}$.

Now, consider the three scientists shown in Fig. 1 that have been extracted from the DBpedia repository[1]. By relying on conventional linked data matching and clustering approaches, we evaluate the degree of similarity of the three scientists by considering all their properties [7]. We obtain that Thacker and Culler are similar since they have been both affiliated at the University of California in Berkeley, while Thacker and Iverson are similar since they received the Turing Award. These two pairs of resources have the same degree of similarity, in that they have the same number of matching properties (i.e., almaMater and award, respectively), though this set is completely different for the two pairs. Using such similarities with a conventional hierarchical clustering algorithm [25], the three scientists are placed into one single cluster (see Fig. 2(a)). However, by exploring the contents of this cluster, it is difficult to recognize the *cause of similarity* that generated the cluster, since the elements therein contained are similar on different properties.

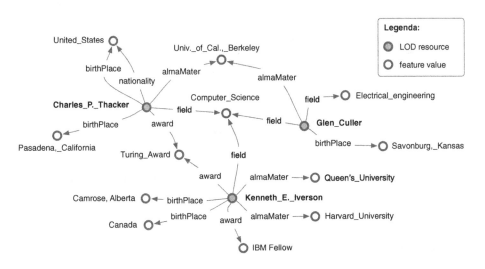

Fig. 1. Example of computer scientists from DBpedia

---

[1] For the sake of readability, only a subset of the available properties is reported (http://www.dbpedia.org).

A distinguishing feature of dimensional clustering is the capability to discriminate the so-called **cause of similarity** that generated a cluster. Dimensional clustering performs resource aggregation by taking into account both the degree of similarity and the set of similarity properties. Resources with the same degree of similarity, but different set of similar properties are put in different clusters. As a result, we have that the elements of a cluster obtained through a dimensional clustering are characterized by a common set of similarity properties. In our example, according to dimensional clustering, the three scientists are put in two different clusters for their profession: one containing Thacker and Culler that are characterized by the matching property almaMater, and one containing Thacker and Iverson that match on the property award (see Fig. 2(b)). Instead, by taking into account their geographical features, such as the birthPlace, Thacker, Culler, and Iverson are grouped in three different clusters according to the information available about their place of birth.

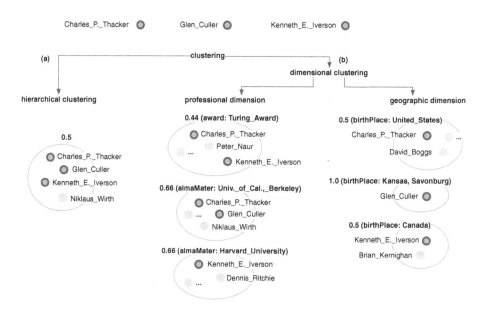

Fig. 2. Example of (a) hierarchical clustering and (b) dimensional clustering

3   Dimensional Data Clustering

Dimensional data clustering enables to generate multiple similarity-based views of a given corpus of linked data based on the use of thematic dimensions (see Fig. 3). The process starts with the definition of the corpus $\mathcal{C}$ extracted from a LOD (Linked Open Data) repository $\mathcal{R}$ (e.g., DBpedia, Freebase). The list of thematic dimensions $\mathcal{D}_1, \ldots, \mathcal{D}_k$ is then specified to describe the different perspectives to consider for dimensional clustering. Matching and clustering are executed to generate the corresponding cluster sets $CL^{\mathcal{D}_1} \ldots CL^{\mathcal{D}_k}$. Ensemble operations are finally invoked to enable a user in combining the single-dimension cluster sets with the goal to generate a multi-dimension cluster set $CL^{\mathcal{D}_{1\ldots k}}$

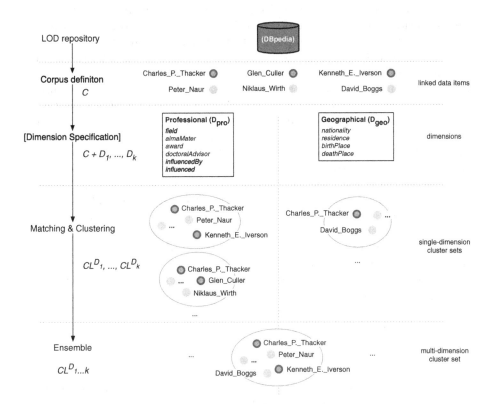

Fig. 3. The process of dimensional data clustering

For dimensional clustering, we stress that corpus definition and dimension specification are executed only once for all the cluster sets to generate. Instead, a specific execution of matching and clustering is required for each thematic dimension $\mathcal{D}_i \in \{\mathcal{D}_1, \ldots, \mathcal{D}_k\}$ to produce a corresponding cluster set $CL^{\mathcal{D}_i} \in CL^{\mathcal{D}_1} \ldots CL^{\mathcal{D}_k}$. Based on single-dimension cluster sets, the user exploits the ensemble operations for interactive, on-the-fly creation of multi-dimension cluster sets.

In the following, we first describe the steps of corpus definition and dimension specification. Matching and clustering techniques are presented in Sects. 4 and 5, respectively. Ensemble operations are finally discussed in Sect. 6.

3.1 Corpus Definition

The corpus C is the dataset of linked data on which dimensional clustering is performed. In line of principle, the corpus can coincide with the entire content of a considered LOD repository R. In the practice, the user is generally interested in a topic-oriented corpus extracted from R through a number of appropriate queries. In this case, the notion of *seed of interest* is introduced for enabling the user to indicate the argument/topic she/he is interested about. Two options are available. As a first option, the seed of interest s can be a linked data URI of R to use as point of origin for extraction. In this case, the extraction retrieves those linked data of R that are pertinent to the seed s, namely those resources that are connected to s through a property path of length $\leq d$. The distance d is a parameter to set the extension at which linked data extraction has to be enforced. The choice of the d parameter has an impact on the number of extracted linked data and thus on the size of the resulting dataset to consider for clustering. In usual scenarios, a distance $d = 2$ is a good trade-off to obtain a well-sized dataset of pertinent linked data about s. As a second option, the seed of interest s can be a keyword. In this case, the extraction retrieves those linked data that have s in a property value. Multiple seeds of interest can be specified by the user to further enlarge the corpus of linked data to consider.

The linked data resources belonging to the corpus C are represented through an internal data model based on the notion of *linked data item (ldi)*, capturing the features of interest for matching and clustering of linked data resources [8]. A ldi captures and properly represents the fact that a linked data is characterized by a set of properties and types through the notion of feature which can have multiple associated values. A ldi is defined as follows:

$$ldi = \{f_1, \ldots, f_n\}$$

For each feature $f_i \in ldi$, a set of *feature values* $V_i = \{v_1, \ldots, v_k\}$ is defined to represent the set of values of the feature f_i.

Given a resource URI_1 extracted from the repository R, the corresponding representation $ldi_1 \in C$ is created as follows[2].

Creation of features from types. For each type t that characterizes URI_1, a feature $f_i = type$ and a corresponding $V_i = \{t\}$ are created in the ldi_1 structure. As an example, consider the linked data resources of Fig. 1. The URI Glen_Culler is characterized by the types Person and ComputerPioneers. The following ldi structure is created:

$$\text{Glen\_Culler} = \{\ldots, type_i, \ldots\}$$

$$V_i = \{\text{Person, ComputerPioneers}\}$$

---

[2] More technical details about the construction of linked data items from the RDF statements of a repository R are provided in [5].

Creation of features from properties. For each pair property/value $\langle p, p_v \rangle$ that is directly connected with URI_1, a feature $f_i = p$ and a corresponding feature value $v_j = p_v$ with $v_j \in V_i$ are created in the ldi structure. When a set of pairs $\{\langle p, p_{v_1} \rangle, \ldots, \langle p, p_{v_k} \rangle\}$ is connected to URI_1 for a given property p, a value v_j is inserted in V_i for each p_{v_h} with $h \in [1, k]$. For example, the URI Glen_Culler is connected to the following set of pairs for the property field: $\{\langle \mathrm{field}, \mathrm{Computer\_Science} \rangle, \langle \mathrm{field}, \mathrm{Electrical\_engineering} \rangle\}$. The following ldi structure is created:

$$\mathrm{Glen\_Culler} = \{\ldots, \mathrm{field}_i, \ldots\}$$

$$V_i = \{\mathrm{Computer\_Science}, \mathrm{Electrical\_engineering}\}$$

The complete ldi representation of the linked data resources of Fig. 1 is presented in Fig. 4.

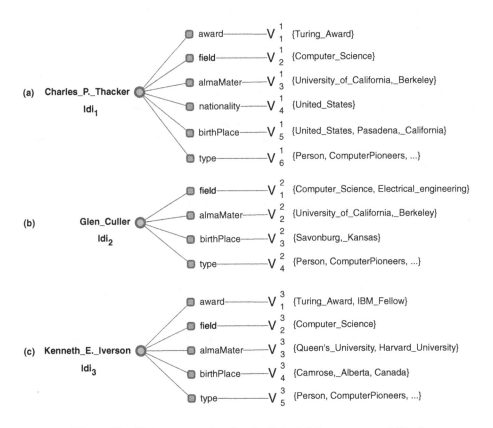

Fig. 4. The ldi representation for the linked data resources of Fig. 1

3.2   Dimension Specification

The specification of a thematic dimension consists in selecting the set of features that are involved in the dimension. In general, the user can specify a thematic dimension by exploiting the list of available features, either properties or types, in the corpus $\mathcal{C}$. In defining a dimension, the user has to tick the features that she/he considers as "distinguishing" in describing the perspective of interest, such as for example the property field for a professional dimension. Furthermore, the specification of a label is required to associate a dimension with an intuitive name that describes the dimension purpose.

As a remark, we stress that features more commonly employed in the corpus $\mathcal{C}$ have a higher impact on dimensional clustering rather than those that are rarely used. This is due to the fact that a thematic dimension determines the features to use for matching and clustering and a feature is important as long as it is present in the ldi structures to match. As a consequence, a few (e.g., three) common features are sufficient to characterize a thematic dimension in most situations.

As a further remark, we note that the step of dimension specification is optional. A number of thematic dimensions can be predefined to cover most common point of views on data. Personal, professional, geographical, and temporal dimensions are examples of predefined dimensions that can be made available to all the interested users as default thematic dimensions. The dimensions $\mathcal{D}_{pro}$ and $\mathcal{D}_{geo}$ of Fig. 3 are examples of **professional** and **geographic** dimensions, respectively. In this scenario, we consider the manual specification of a new thematic dimension as an exceptional event, that occurs when the user has the need to consider peculiar data aspects that are not already captured by the default dimensions. New dimensions are stored and they become available for subsequent executions of dimensional clustering. Dimensions that are non-interesting for the user and/or non-pertaining for the specific corpus at hand can be de-activated.

4   Matching Techniques

Matching linked data for dimensional clustering requires to consider that the similarity evaluation is invoked over a specific thematic dimension. This means that the matching operations focus only on the features belonging to the considered thematic dimension. Leveraging on the ldi structure, we define three different matching functions to enforce matching of linked data at different level of detail. Given a dimension $\mathcal{D}$ and two linked data items ldi_1 and ldi_2, we present:

- The *v-match* function for matching two feature values v_s and v_t.
- The *f-match* function for matching two features f_i and f_j, based on the results of the v-match function over their corresponding feature value sets V_i and V_j.
- The *ldi-match* function for determining a comprehensive similarity value of two linked data items ldi_1 and ldi_2 based on the results of the f-match function over their features involved in the thematic dimension $\mathcal{D}$.

The v-match function. The function v-match() $\rightarrow [0, 1]$ is defined to compare two feature values v_s and v_t. According to the linked data paradigm, we observe that a feature value can be a basic datatype value (e.g., a string, a number, a date) or a resource (i.e., URI). When v_s and v_t are basic datatype values, v-match is calculated through an appropriate function depending on the specific datatype format. For instance, techniques for approximate string matching like I-Sub, Q-Gram, Edit-distance, and Jaro-Winkler, can be employed when string values are involved [17]. In case that v_s and v_t are resources, v-match is defined as follows:

$$\text{v-match}(v_s, v_t) = \begin{cases} 1 \text{ if } v_s \equiv v_t \\ 0 \text{ otherwise} \end{cases}$$

This means that v-match returns 1 when the values v_s and v_t reference the same resource, and 0 otherwise.

The f-match function. The function f-match() $\rightarrow [0, 1]$ is defined to compare two features f_i and f_j by relying on the v-match function to determine the number of matching values in V_i and V_j. To this end, a *best matching* strategy is enforced. This means that for each element of V_i, the element in V_j with the highest matching result is considered for feature matching evaluation. The f-match function is calculated as follows:

$$\text{f-match}(f_i, f_j) = \frac{\sum_{s=1}^{k} max(\text{v-match}(v_s, v_t)) \ \forall t \in [1, h]}{k}$$

where $v_s \in V_i$, $v_t \in V_j$, $k = |V_i|$, and $h = |V_j|$. The choice to use best matching instead of a more common strategy based on Dice/Jaccard coefficients is motivated by the fact that usually the cardinalities $|V_i|$ and $|V_j|$ are different. In such a case, Dice/Jaccard coefficients consider the absence of values to compare as mismatching values, thus producing lower matching results than the best matching strategy. Furthermore, we stress that the above f-match function is not symmetric, meaning that f-match $(f_i, f_j) \neq$ f-match(f_j, f_i) when $k \neq h$. To overcome this situation, we always consider as first argument of f-match the feature with the lower number of values between V_i and V_j. As a result, given f_i and f_j to match, we calculate f-match (f_i, f_j) when $k \leq h$ and f-match (f_j, f_i) otherwise.

As an **example**, we consider the feature award of ldi_1 and ldi_3, and the corresponding feature values V_1^1 and V_1^3 of Fig. 4(a) and (c), respectively. Since V_1^1 has less values than V_1^3, we set V_1^1 as first argument when invoking f-match. Through the v-match function, we find that V_1^1 has a corresponding matching value in V_1^3 (i.e., Turing_Award). Thus, we have:

$$\text{f-match}(\text{award}, \text{award}) = \frac{1}{1} = 1.0$$

The ldi-match function. The function ldi-match() $\rightarrow [0, 1]$ is defined to produce a comprehensive similarity value between two linked data items ldi_1 and

ldi_2 according to a given thematic dimension $\mathcal{D}$. The result of the ldi-match function is calculated by relying on the f-match function and it is based on the similarity between the features of ldi_1 and ldi_2 that belong to the thematic dimension $\mathcal{D}$. The ldi-match function along a dimension $\mathcal{D}$ is calculated as follows:

$$\text{ldi-match}^{\mathcal{D}}(ldi_1, ldi_2) = \frac{\sum_{i=1}^{n} \sum_{j=1}^{m} \text{f-match}(f_i, f_j)}{n}$$

where $f_i, f_j \in \mathcal{D}$, $f_i \in ldi_1$, $f_j \in ldi_2$, $n = |ldi_1|$, and $m = |ldi_2|$. For optimization purposes, we stress that only corresponding features of ldi_1 and ldi_2 are matched (i.e., $f_i = f_j$), while non-corresponding features are discarded. This means that f-match is invoked on the features of ldi_1 and ldi_2 that have the same URI within the considered thematic dimension $\mathcal{D}$. As for the f-match function, we calculate ldi-match$^{\mathcal{D}}(ldi_1, ldi_2)$ when $n \leq m$ and ldi-match$^{\mathcal{D}}(ldi_2, ldi_1)$ otherwise.

As an **example**, we calculate ldi-match$^{\mathcal{D}_{pro}}(\mathsf{ldi}_1, \mathsf{ldi}_3)$ for the items of Fig. 4 (i.e., Charles P. Thacker and Kenneth E. Iverson, respectively) and the thematic dimension $\mathcal{D}_{pro}$ of Fig. 3. To this end, we first calculate f-match for the corresponding features of ldi_1 and ldi_3 (i.e., $f_i = f_j$ with $f_i \in \mathsf{ldi}_1$ and $f_j \in \mathsf{ldi}_3$). Thus, we have:

$$\text{f-match}(\mathsf{award}, \mathsf{award}) = \frac{1}{1} = 1$$

$$\text{f-match}(\mathsf{almaMater}, \mathsf{almaMater}) = \frac{0}{1} = 0$$

$$\text{f-match}(\mathsf{field}, \mathsf{field}) = \frac{1}{1} = 1$$

For the calculation of f-match($\mathsf{award}, \mathsf{award}$), we observe that the set V_1^1 of Fig. 4 is used as first argument of the function f-match according to our symmetrization mechanism. As a final result, we obtain:

$$\text{ldi-match}^{\mathcal{D}_{pro}}(\mathsf{ldi}_1, \mathsf{ldi}_3) = \frac{1 + 0 + 1}{3} = 0.66$$

5   Clustering Techniques

Data clustering is enforced through the algorithm HC^{f+}, a hierarchical clustering algorithm of agglomerative type based on feature similarity of ldis. Agglomerative refers to the fact that clusters are obtained through a series of successive merging operations over ldis. Hierarchical refers to the fact that groups of similar ldis are organized into a tree according to decreasing matching values of ldis starting from the tree leafs up to the root. Given a considered thematic dimension $\mathcal{D}$, the algorithm HC^{f+} produces a cluster set $CL^{\mathcal{D}}$ as a result. Each cluster $cl \in CL^{\mathcal{D}}$ is associated with a similarity coefficient σcl and a set of similarity features πcl. When a single-link strategy is adopted [25], σcl represents the maximum matching value over the dimension $\mathcal{D}$ between any pair of ldis belonging to the cluster cl. With a *complete-link* strategy, σcl denotes the minimum matching value over the dimension $\mathcal{D}$ between any pair of ldis in cl. Furthermore, with respect to the classical algorithm for hierarchical clustering, HC^{f+} presents the following distinguishing aspects:

- *Capability to keep track of the causes of similarity.* With HC^{f+}, the feature set πcl is introduced which contains those ldi features of $\mathcal{D}$ that match for the items of cl. In other words, πcl lists the ldi features that generate cl in the thematic dimension $\mathcal{D}$ and it represents the "motivation" for which cl has been created.
- *Support to overlapping clusters.* With HC^{f+}, a certain ldi can belong to more than one cluster depending on its similarity with the cluster items over πcl. A ldi_1 can be placed in two clusters cl_1 and cl_2 having different set s πcl_1 and πcl_2. This is due to the fact that ldi_1 can match with the ldis of cl_1 on the features πcl_1 and with the ldis of cl_2 on the features πcl_2, at the same time.

In the following, we rely on the complete-link strategy that produces a higher number of smaller clusters than the single-link strategy due to the fact that a minimum level of similarity is ensured between any pair ldis in a cluster. Such an effect is well-suited for linked data aggregation where cluster homogeneity is an important property for the overall relevance of the resulting clustering $CL^{\mathcal{D}}$ (see the experimental results of Sect. 8).

Consider a thematic dimension $\mathcal{D}$ and a corpus $\mathcal{C}$ of ldis to be clustered. For HC^{f+} calculation, we define a similarity matrix σM where an element $\sigma M[i,j] = \text{ldi-match}^{\mathcal{D}}(ldi_i, ldi_j)$ represents the ldi-match value computed between the items ldi_i and ldi_j along the dimension $\mathcal{D}$. Moreover, we also define the feature matrix πM where an element $\pi M[i,j] \subseteq \mathcal{D}$ is a set containing the similarity features of ldi_i and ldi_j[3]. The hierarchical clustering algorithm HC^{f+} is shown in Algorithm 1. Let $k = |\mathcal{C}|$ be the size of the corpus $\mathcal{C}$. A singleton cluster cl_r is created for each $ldi_r \in \mathcal{C}$. Initially, $\sigma cl_r = 1$ and $\pi cl_r = \mathcal{D}$. The two clusters cl_i and cl_j (with $i \neq j$) having the highest matching value in σM are selected and merged in a cluster cl_k with $\sigma cl_k = \sigma M[i,j]$ and $\pi cl_k = \pi M[i,j]$. A new line and column of order k is inserted in both σM and πM for the cluster cl_k. The elements $\sigma M[z,k]$ and $\pi M[z,k]$ are then calculated to determine the similarity value and the set of similarity features between the new cluster cl_k and each element z of σM and πM, respectively. In detail, according to the complete-link strategy, $\sigma M[z,k]$ is the lower value between $\sigma M[z,i]$ and $\sigma M[z,j]$, while $\pi M[z,k]$ is the set of similarity features in common among $\pi M[z,i]$, $\pi M[z,j]$, and πcl_k. We stress that $\sigma M[z,k]$ is set to zero when $\pi M[z,k] = \emptyset$. Two clusters are candidate/considered for merging in HC^{f+} only if they have a non-empty set of common similarity features in πM. Finally, the σM matrix is cleared by setting to zero all those elements that are irrelevant for the merge operations of further clusters. An element $\sigma M[i,k]$ is irrelevant when the corresponding set of similarity features $\pi M[i,k]$ is a subset of $\pi M[i,j]$, meaning that the cluster cl_k

---

[3] Since ldi-match$^{\mathcal{D}}(ldi_i, ldi_j) = \text{ldi-match}^{\mathcal{D}}(ldi_j, ldi_i)$, we define σM and πM as upper triangular matrices.

already considers the features in $\pi M[i, k]$. Analogously, the element $\sigma M[k, j]$ can be irrelevant and thus cleared from the matrix σM. The clustering algorithm terminates when the σM is a zero matrix. The ending condition is guaranteed by the fact that the elements of σM are progressively set to zero.

Algorithm 1. The HC^{f+} clustering algorithm

Input: $\mathcal{C}, \mathcal{D}, \sigma M, \pi M$
Output: $CL^{\mathcal{D}}$
2: $\quad k \leftarrow size(\mathcal{C})$

4: **for all** $ldi_r \in \mathcal{C}$ **do** $\qquad\qquad\qquad\qquad\qquad$ ▷ Creation of a new cluster
$\qquad$ Create a cluster $cl_r \leftarrow \{ldi_r\}$
6: $\qquad \sigma cl_r \leftarrow 1$
$\qquad \pi cl_r \leftarrow \mathcal{D}$
8: **end for**

10: **repeat**
$\qquad (i, j) \leftarrow$ position of the greatest value in σM (with $i \neq j$)
12: $\qquad$ Create new cluster $cl_k \leftarrow cl_i \cup cl_j$
$\qquad \sigma cl_k \leftarrow \sigma M[i, j]$
14: $\qquad \pi cl_k \leftarrow \pi M[i, j]$

16: $\qquad$ Create new line and column k in σM and πM

18: $\qquad$ **for** $z = 0 \rightarrow k$ **do**
$\qquad\qquad \pi M[z, k] \leftarrow \pi M[z, i] \cap \pi M[z, j] \cap \pi cl_k$
20: $\qquad\qquad$ **if** $\pi M[z, k] \neq \emptyset$ **then**
$\qquad\qquad\qquad \sigma M[z, k] \leftarrow min(\sigma M[z, i], \sigma M[z, j])$
22: $\qquad\qquad$ **else**
$\qquad\qquad\qquad \sigma M[z, k] \leftarrow 0$
24: $\qquad\qquad$ **end if**
$\qquad$ **end for** $\qquad\qquad\qquad\qquad\qquad\qquad\qquad$ ▷ Clearing of σM
26: $\qquad$ **for all** $z \leq k$ **do**
$\qquad\qquad$ **if** $\pi M[i, k] \subseteq \pi M[i, j]$ **then**
28: $\qquad\qquad\qquad \sigma M[i, k] \leftarrow 0$
$\qquad\qquad$ **end if**
30:
$\qquad\qquad$ **if** $\pi M[k, j] \subseteq \pi M[i, j]$ **then**
32: $\qquad\qquad\qquad \sigma M[k, j] \leftarrow 0$
$\qquad\qquad$ **end if**
34: $\qquad$ **end for**

36: $\qquad k \leftarrow k + 1$

38: **until** σM is a zero matrix

As an **example** of HC^{f+}, we take into account the ldis of Fig. 4. According to the features of dimension $\mathcal{D}_{pro}$, the similarity matrix among the resources is shown in Fig. 5, with ldi_1 = Charles_P._Thacker, ldi_2 = Glen_Culler, and ldi_3 = Kenneth_E._Iverson. Given the similarity values of Fig. 5, a classic hierarchical clustering procedure using the complete-link strategy will end up with a single cluster including all the three ldis. In fact, in the first step the similarity value $\sigma M[ldi_1, ldi_2] = 1.0$ between Thacker and Culler is selected and ldi_1 and ldi_2 are included in a cluster. Subsequently, the matrix is updated and the value of similarity between the new cluster and the resource ldi_3 is calculated as the minimum similarity between ldi_3 and ldi_1 and ldi_3 and ldi_2, which is equal to 0.5. Then, according to this approach, ldi_3 will also be included in the same cluster containing ldi_1 and ldi_2. Instead, HC^{f+} produces two different clusters containing Thacker, Culler on one side and Thacker and Iverson on the other side, due to their different causes of similarity. In detail, we initially select the similarity value $\sigma M[ldi_1, ldi_2] = 1.0$ and we create a cluster cl_1 containing ldi_1 and ldi_2. This cluster is associated with a set of features $\pi cl_1 = \pi M[ldi_1, ldi_2] = \{field, almaMater\}$ corresponding to the similarity features between Thacker and Culler. Then, we take into account the similarity between the new cluster cl_1 and ldi_3 and we try to insert the resource ldi_3 into cl_1. In doing this, we consider the intersection between the labeling features πcl_1 and the matching features between ldi_3 and the items of cl_1, that are $\pi M[ldi_1, ldi_3] = \{field\}$. Thus, ldi_3 cannot be inserted in the cluster because the field feature is not matching. Thus, we consider the similarity between Thacker and Iverson and we create a second cluster labeled with the features award and field. The final result is the creation of two clusters, one describing computer scientists who won the Turing Award (i.e., Thacker and Iverson), the other describing computer scientists who worked in the University of Berkeley (i.e., Thacker and Culler), as shown in Fig. 2.

	ldi_1	ldi_2	ldi_3
ldi_1	1.0	1.0	0.66
ldi_2		1.0	0.5
ldi_3			1.0

Fig. 5. Similarity matrix for Charles_P._Thacker, Glen_Culler, and Kenneth_E._Iverson

6   Ensemble of Dimensional Cluster Sets

Clusters sets of different thematic dimensions can be mixed up to provide a sort of "multi-dimension" view of the underlying corpus of ldis. To this end, we introduce the *ensemble operation* to enforce the combination of different dimensional cluster sets obtained over a given corpus of ldis.

Cluster-set ensemble. Given two dimensional cluster sets $CL^{\mathcal{D}_1}$ and $CL^{\mathcal{D}_2}$ over a corpus of linked data items $\mathcal{C}$, ensemble is the merge operation that generates a multi-dimension cluster set $CL^{\mathcal{D}_{12}}$ by combining the clusters of $CL^{\mathcal{D}_1}$ and $CL^{\mathcal{D}_2}$, respectively.

In line of principle, a multi-dimension cluster set can be generated from scratch by considering the whole set of features belonging to all the different thematic dimensions when performing matching and clustering. As an example based on Fig. 3, if we are interested in generating a cluster set based on both personal and professional features, we can apply the dimensional clustering approach of Sect. 3 by considering a thematic dimension $\mathcal{D} = \mathcal{D}_1 \cup \mathcal{D}_2$. Although this is always possible, using ensemble has two main advantages. First, ensemble enables the generation on-the-fly of a multi-dimension cluster set in a flexible and rapid way, by relying on already-available single-dimension cluster sets. Second, ensemble allows to select the dimensions to be considered for merging cluster sets, thus enabling the construction of different and personalized similarity views of the underlying corpus of ldis in a bottom-up fashion.

Given two dimensional cluster sets $CL^{\mathcal{D}_1}$ and $CL^{\mathcal{D}_2}$, ensemble requires the definition of:

– *set operations*, to specify how to merge the items in two selected clusters;
– *criteria*, to determine which pairs of clusters $\langle cl_i, cl_j \rangle$ are candidate for merging in two cluster sets $CL^{\mathcal{D}_1}$ and $CL^{\mathcal{D}_2}$, respectively;
– *policies*, to handle the situation of multiple candidate clusters $cl_j \in CL^{\mathcal{D}_2}$ identified for a given cluster $cl_i \in CL^{\mathcal{D}_1}$.

6.1   Ensemble Set Operations

The goal of set operations is to create a multi-dimension cluster $cl_k \in CL^{\mathcal{D}_{12}}$ out of the items belonging to the two clusters $cl_i \in CL^{\mathcal{D}_1}$ and $cl_j \in CL^{\mathcal{D}_2}$. Basically, the classical *cluster union*, *cluster intersection*, and *cluster difference* set operations can be employed to this end.

Cluster union. The cluster cl_k is created by including the linked data items that belong to either cl_i or cl_j (i.e., $cl_k = cl_i \cup cl_j$). This operation generates a multi-dimension cluster cl_k that provides a sort of "this or that" similarity view of the items of the single-dimension clusters cl_i and cl_j. As an example, consider the clusters cl_i and cl_j of Fig. 6 about computer scientists who won the Turing Award and scientists from the United States, respectively. Merging cl_i and cl_j; the union operation creates a cluster representing scientists who won the Turing Award or from the United States.

Cluster intersection. The cluster cl_k is created by including the linked data items that belong to both cl_i and cl_j (i.e., $cl_k = cl_i \cap cl_j$). This operation generates a multi-dimension cluster cl_k that provides a sort of "this and that" similarity view of the items of the single-dimension clusters cl_i and cl_j. With respect to the example of Fig. 6, the merged cluster obtained through the intersection operation represents scientists from United States who won the Turing Award.

Cluster difference. The cluster cl_k is created by including the linked data items that belong to cl_i but not to cl_j (i.e., $cl_k = cl_i \backslash cl_j$). This operation generates a multi-dimension cluster cl_k that provides a sort of "this but not that" similarity view of the items of the single-dimension clusters cl_i and cl_j. With respect to the example of Fig. 6, the merged cluster obtained through the difference operation represents scientists who won the Turing Award that are from outside the United States.

Cluster-intersection is set as the default ensemble set operation. However, we expect that the choice of the ensemble set operation is manually performed by the user according to the kind of combination that she/he aims to highlight in the resulting multi-dimension cluster set.

Example. As an example of the three ensemble set operations, we suppose to merge the first two dimensional clusters of Fig. 2. The results of the three ensemble set operations are shown in Fig. 6.

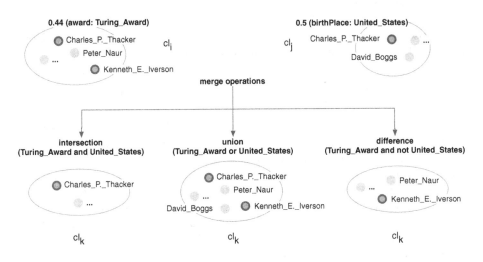

Fig. 6. Example of the ensemble set operations

6.2 Ensemble Criteria

The goal of ensemble criteria is to determine the pairs of candidate clusters to merge. In the literature about cluster ensemble, most of the existing techniques for candidate detection are based on cluster overlaps. The idea is that the higher is the number of common items between two clusters, the more the two clusters are good candidate for merging [13,21]. However, the cluster overlap alone is recognized as not adequate to all the situations, such as for example when the number of common items is high for the majority of clusters in the considered cluster sets [10]. Moreover, the overlap can be related to items that are marginal for the considered clusters, thus resulting in candidate clusters that are poorly meaningful. For this reason, in the following, we propose three different criteria for detecting the pairs of clusters that are candidate for merging, namely *centrality-driven*, *mutuality-driven*, and *user-driven* criteria. For each criterion, given a cluster $cl_i \in CL^{\mathcal{D}_1}$, the goal is to find the set $cand(cl_i)$ of *merge-candidate clusters* containing those clusters $cl_j \in CL^{\mathcal{D}_2}$ suggested for merging.

Centrality-driven criterion. This criterion relies on the notion of *representative items* to determine the candidate clusters to merge. Given a cluster $cl_i \in CL^{\mathcal{D}_1}$, the representative items $RI(cl_i)$ of cl_i is a set containing the items of cl_i with the highest similarity value within cl_i according to the ldi-match function, namely:

$$RI(cl_i) = \{ldi_k \in cl_i \mid MAX[\text{ldi-match}^{\mathcal{D}_1}(ldi_k, ldi_h)], \forall ldi_h \in cl_i, \ k \neq h\}$$

The set $RI(cl_i)$ can contain two or more items, depending on the number of item pairs whose degree of similarity is equal to $MAX[\text{ldi-match}^{\mathcal{D}_1}(ldi_k, ldi_h)]$. Given a cluster $cl_i \in CL^{\mathcal{D}_1}$, the set of its merge-candidate clusters $cand(cl_i)$ is composed by those clusters of $CL^{\mathcal{D}_2}$ having the highest number of common representative items with cl_i (based on the Jaccard coefficient), that is:

$$cand(cl_i) = \{cl_j \mid \frac{\mid RI(cl_i) \cap RI(cl_j) \mid}{\mid RI(cl_i) \cup RI(cl_j) \mid} \geq th_r\}$$

where $cl_j \in CL^{\mathcal{D}_2}$ and th_r is the minimum threshold of common representative items required to a pair of clusters for being candidate to merge. The th_r value is defined during setup to configure the behavior of ensemble criteria. A high threshold value (i.e., $0.6 \leq th_r \leq 0.9$) is set when a *highly-selective approach* to the specification of candidate clusters is enforced, in that only clusters with the same or very similar representative items are considered for merging. On the opposite, a low threshold value (i.e., $0.2 \leq th_r \leq 0.5$) is set when a *loosely-selective approach* is enforced, in that also clusters with poorly similar representative items are considered for merging.

The centrality-driven criterion is the default criterion for defining the set of candidate clusters to merge. In particular, this criterion is particularly appropriate when clusters have low homogeneity, meaning that some items are more relevant/central than others for a considered cluster.

Mutuality-driven criterion. This criterion is borrowed from the notion of *adjusted mutual information*, conceived for comparing two sets of clusters built over the same corpus of items [19]. Given two random variables, mutual information measures how much knowing one of these two variables reduces the uncertainty about the other. This property suggests that the mutual information can be used to measure the information shared by two cluster sets, and thus, assess their similarity. To this end, we first introduce the measure $p(i)$, that is the probability of a cluster $cl_i \in CL^{\mathcal{D}_1}$. Suppose to pick an item at random from the corpus $\mathcal{C}$, then the probability that the item belongs to cl_i is:

$$p(i) = \frac{\mid cl_i \mid}{\mid \mathcal{C} \mid}$$

where $|\mathcal{C}|$ is the cardinality of the corpus $\mathcal{C}$. According to this, we introduce the notion of *ensemble degree* that captures the mutual interdependence of two clusters belonging to different cluster sets. Given a cluster $cl_i \in CL^{\mathcal{D}_1}$ and a cluster $cl_j \in CL^{\mathcal{D}_2}$, the ensemble degree $I(cl_i, cl_j)$ is calculated as:

$$I(cl_i, cl_j) = p(i, j) \log \frac{p(i, j)}{p(i)p'(j)}$$

where $p'(j) = |cl_j|/|\mathcal{C}|$ and $p(i, j)$ is the probability that a randomly picked item belongs to both cl_i and cl_j and it is calculated as:

$$p(i, j) = \frac{|cl_i \cap cl_j|}{|\mathcal{C}|}$$

According to the mutuality-driven criterion, the pairs of clusters with the higher mutual information are candidate for merging. To this end, given a cluster $cl_i \in CL^{\mathcal{D}_1}$, the set of its merge-candidate clusters $cand(cl_i)$ is defined as:

$$cand(cl_i) = \{cl_j \mid I(cl_i, cl_j) \geq th_i\}$$

where $cl_j \in CL^{\mathcal{D}_2}$ and th_i is a threshold defined to set the minimum level of mutual information required to a pair of clusters for being candidate to merge.

The mutuality-driven criterion builds candidate clusters to merge on the basis of their overlap. With respect to a simple metric based on a Jaccard coefficient to measure this degree of overlap, our criterion based on mutual information is more accurate, especially in those situations where the portion of overlapping items is high [10]. As a general remark, we note that the mutuality-driven criterion is appropriate when the goal is to merge clusters that have "something in common" without being interested in the relevance/centrality of the overlapping items with respect to the cluster they belong to. Thus, the mutuality-driven criterion is recommended when clusters have high homogeneity, meaning that, given a cluster, the relevance of the items therein contained is more or less the same for all the cluster items.

User-driven criterion. The problem of detecting the pairs of clusters to merge can also be addressed through a manual procedure. For cluster ensemble, the user can browse two cluster sets $CL^{\mathcal{D}_1}$ and $CL^{\mathcal{D}_2}$ with the goal to manually choose the pairs of clusters to merge according to her/his personal interests/knowledge. Such a basic approach is always possible and it is suggested when the user is interested in combining clusters according to a specific user-defined requirement. In this case, given a cluster $cl_i \in CL^{\mathcal{D}_1}$, the set of merge-candidate clusters $cand(cl_i)$ is defined as the set of clusters $cl_j \in CL^{\mathcal{D}_2}$ that are manually selected by the user for possible merge. When large cluster sets with a high number of clusters are considered, the manual choice of the cluster pairs to merge can be difficult and ineffective. In this case, the use of automated criteria, such as the mutuality-driven and the centrality-driven criteria, are well-suited alternatives to obtain a set of candidate pairs of clusters to merge.

Example. As an example, we consider the cluster cl_i obtained for the geo-graphical dimension ($\mathcal{D}_{geo}$), which contains the items representing David_Boggs, Charles_P._Thacker, Donald_Knuth, Douglas_Engelbart, Stephen_Cole_Kleene, Jack_Kilby, that are computer scientists born in the United States. Starting from cl_i, we apply both the centrality-driven and the mutuality-driven criteria in order to find a ordered list of candidates for merging in the cluster set of the professional dimension $\mathcal{D}_{pro}$. The results of the two criteria are shown in Fig. 7, where we report the set $cand(cl_i)$ and we highlight in bold the common items between the starting cluster cl_i and the candidates. The example shows that the centrality-driven criterion produces a smaller number of candidates than the mutuality-driven one. The candidates produced by the centrality criterion cor-respond to the top-5 clusters produced with mutuality. In fact, since mutuality is less dependent from the most relevant items in the clusters, it considers as candidates also clusters that are quite large even if they do not contain relevant items.

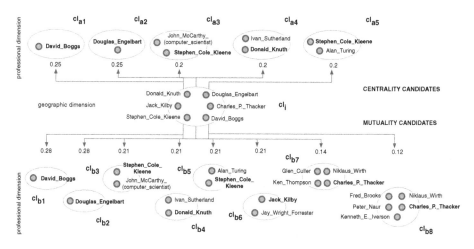

Fig. 7. Merge-candidate for cluster cl_i according to the centrality-driven and mutuality-driven criteria

6.3   Ensemble Merge Policies

The goal of ensemble policies is to define how to exploit the candidates to merge. In detail, the ensemble policy defines how to merge a cluster $cl_i \in CL^{\mathcal{D}_1}$ with the cluster(s) in $cand(cl_i)$. If $cand(cl_i)$ contains more than one candidate cluster, different options are possible. An option is to choose only one cluster in $cand(cl_i)$ as the best candidate to use for merging operation (*one-to-one* policy). Another option is to merge the cluster cl_i with all the candidates in $cand(cl_i)$ (*one-to-many* policy).

One-to-one policy. In this policy, only the "best" candidate cluster $cl_j \in cand(cl_i)$ is selected for merging with the cluster $cl_i \in CL^{\mathcal{D}_1}$. In the centrality-driven criterion, for a cluster $cl_i \in CL^{\mathcal{D}_1}$, the best candidate is the cluster $cl_j \in cand(cl_i)$ with the highest Jaccard coefficient calculated on the sets of representative items $RI(cl_i)$ and $RI(cl_j)$, respectively. In the mutuality-driven criterion, the best candidate is the cluster maximizing the value of mutual information $I(cl_i, cl_j)$. In case more than one best candidate is retrieved, we merge cl_i with all the best candidates in one single cluster. The one-to-one policy generates a multi-dimension cluster set with a prefixed maximum number of clusters in it. Given the cluster sets $CL^{\mathcal{D}_1}$ and $CL^{\mathcal{D}_2}$, the multi-dimension cluster set $CL^{\mathcal{D}_{12}}$ generated through the one-to-one policy is such that:

$$| CL^{\mathcal{D}_{12}} | \leq | CL^{\mathcal{D}_1} |$$

In particular, $|CL^{\mathcal{D}_{12}}| = |CL^{\mathcal{D}_1}|$ when at least one merge-candidate cluster exists for each cluster $cl_i \in CL^{\mathcal{D}_1}$ (i.e., $|cand(cl_i)| \geq 1$, $\forall cl_i \in CL^{\mathcal{D}_1}$). A cluster $cl_i \in CL^{\mathcal{D}_1}$ without merge-candidates is not considered for ensemble. In such a case, $|CL^{\mathcal{D}_{12}}| < |CL^{\mathcal{D}_1}|$. Thus, we observe that the resulting multi-dimension cluster set $CL^{\mathcal{D}_{12}}$ is equivalent (or smaller) in size (i.e., number of clusters) with respect to the single-dimension cluster set $CL^{\mathcal{D}_1}$.

The one-to-one policy is well-suited when we are interested in a selective approach where only the most-interesting merge possibility of a cluster cl_i is generated in the resulting multi-dimension cluster set.

One-to-many policy. In this policy, all the merge-candidate clusters $cl_j \in cand(cl_i)$ are considered for merging with the cluster $cl_i \in CL^{\mathcal{D}_1}$. Estimating the size of a multi-dimension cluster set generated through the one-to-many policy is not possible since it depends on the number of candidate clusters $|cand(cl_i)|$ for each cl_i. In general, we observe that the one-to-many policy generates a multi-dimension cluster set $CL^{\mathcal{D}_{12}}$ larger in size with respect to the single-dimension cluster set $CL^{\mathcal{D}_1}$. This is due to the fact that most of the clusters $cl_i \in CL^{\mathcal{D}_1}$ have more than one candidate cluster in $cand(cl_i)$ (especially when the mutuality-driven criterion is adopted).

The one-to-many policy is the default ensemble policy and it is well-suited when we are interested in a conservative approach, assuming that all the candidate clusters $cand(cl_i)$ are potentially-interesting merge possibilities for a cluster cl_i and it is valuable to generate all of them in the resulting multi-dimension cluster set.

Example. As an example of merge policies, we consider the cluster cl_i and the candidates shown in Fig. 7. In the one-to-one policy with the centrality-driven ensemble criterion, cl_i is merged with cl_{a1} and cl_{a2} and a single cluster is generated as a result since both cl_{a1} and cl_{a2} have the same number of representative items. On the opposite, in the one-to-many policy with the mutuality-driven ensemble criterion, cl_i is merged with each cluster $cl_{b1} \ldots cl_{b8}$ and eight clusters are generated as a result.

7   Application to Linked Data Exploration

In this section, we envisage summarization and exploration mechanisms for effective presentation/analysis of a cluster set CL obtained through dimensional clustering and/or ensemble techniques over a considered linked data set of interest.

7.1   Linked Data Summarization

Summarization deals with the problem to provide a high-level, easy-to-read *summary-view* of a given cluster set CL, either single-dimension created through matching/clustering or multi-dimension created through ensemble. To this end, summarization consists in *cluster essential definition, proximity-link specification,* and *prominence value calculation*[4].

Cluster essential definition. A cluster essential $d_i = \langle TAG_i, TYPE_i \rangle$ is a keyword-based summary associated with a cluster cl_i to provide a bird-eye view of the linked data items therein contained. TAG_i is the set of top-occurring tags extracted from the feature values of the ldis belonging to the cluster cl_i, while $TYPE_i$ is the set of types featuring the ldis of cl_i. A cluster essential d_i is represented as a square box attached to the corresponding cluster cl_i.

Proximity-link specification. A proximity link $e(cl_i, cl_j)$ is an interconnection between a pair of clusters $cl_i, cl_j \in CL$ that is specified to denote a thematic relationship between the contents of the two clusters. The proximity link $e(cl_i, cl_j)$ is set when the two clusters cl_i and cl_j have a similar content, based on the number of common ldis. A *degree of proximity* x_{ij} is associated with $e(cl_i, cl_j)$ to express the strength of such a relationship and it is proportional to the overlap (i.e., intersection) between the contents of the clusters cl_i and cl_j. A proximity link $e(cl_i, cl_j)$ is represented as an edge between the clusters cl_i and cl_j. The higher is the degree of proximity x_{ij}, the stronger is the thickness of the associated proximity link $e(cl_i, cl_j)$.

Prominence value calculation. A prominence value p_i is associated with a cluster cl_i to express its importance within the overall cluster set CL. The prominence value p_i is calculated as the betweenness/centrality of the associated cluster cl_i with respect to the cluster set CL. Betweenness is calculated by counting how often the cl_i is traversed by a random walk between two other clusters of CL, using proximity links as path [18]. The higher is the prominence value of a cluster cl_i, the higher is the size of cl_i to better capture the user attention on such a cluster.

An example of summary-view for the multi-dimension cluster set $CL^{\mathcal{D}_{12}}$ is provided in Fig. 8.

---

[4] A detailed presentation of summarization techniques is out of the scope of this work. Here, we outline how to generate a summary-view over a cluster set CL. For the interested reader, a more technical presentation of cluster essential definition, proximity-link specification, and prominence value calculation is provided in [5].

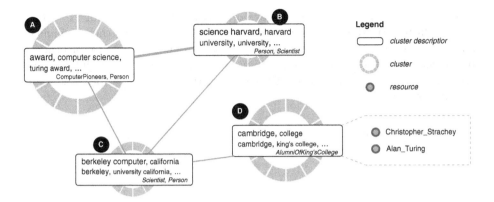

Fig. 8. Example of summary-view for the multi-dimension cluster set $CL^{\mathcal{D}_{12}}$

7.2 Linked Data Exploration

Exploration aims at supporting mechanisms to the user for effectively browsing a cluster set CL based on summary views. Three different mechanisms
can be envisaged that can be switched-on according to the specific user preferences, namely *exploration-by-topic*, *exploration-by-prominence*, and *exploration-
by-proximity*.

Exploration-by-topic. This is the most intuitive exploration mechanism and
it is based on cluster essentials. An essential can be considered as a sort of
instantaneous picture of the associated cluster and linked data items therein
contained, thus allowing the user to rapidly choose the most preferred one for
starting the exploration and/or to execute a keyword search over clusters in
order to find those that contain items of interest. Once selected a cluster of
interest, a preview of the contained linked data is shown to the user for final
data visualization (see the example of Fig. 9(a)).

Exploration-by-prominence. This mechanism allows the user to organize the
exploration according to the prominence values associated with the clusters. The
idea is to support the user in browsing throughout the clusters according to their
relative importance with respect to the entire cluster set. In this mechanism, the
cluster essentials are shown in a sort of tag-cloud (see the example of Fig. 9(b)).
Moreover, clusters are ranked, according to their prominence, from the most
prominent to the less prominent one. By selecting a term of interest in the tag-
cloud, a preview of the associated linked data are shown to the user.

Exploration-by-proximity. This mechanism enables the user to move from
one cluster to another one by exploiting the proximity links. When a user is
exploring a certain cluster, the proximity links provide indication of its
fully/partially overlapping neighbors, thus suggesting the possible exploration
of clusters that are somehow related in content. This mechanism can be coupled either with exploration-by-topic and exploration-by-prominence. Once that

an element of interest is selected for exploration by the user, the links to other related clusters are shown. The degree of proximity that features each proximity link is used to rank the possible exploration paths from one cluster to the others. In particular, in the example of Fig. 9(c), the link labeled "view neighbors" is used in order to access the ranked list of clusters that have a proximity link with the cluster at hand.

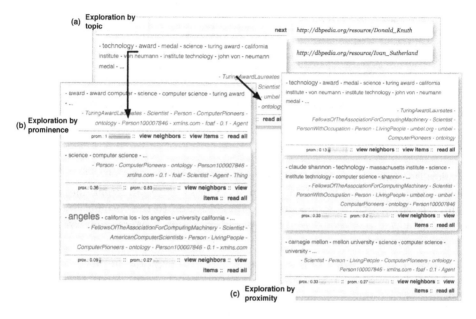

Fig. 9. Examples of exploration mechanisms based on the summary-view of Fig. 8

8   Experimental Evaluation

The goal of our experimental evaluation is twofold: (i) to evaluate the quality of our single-dimension cluster sets when compared against the classical hierarchical clustering approach; (ii) to evaluate the quality of the multi-dimension cluster sets produced through the proposed ensemble techniques.

8.1   Experimental Setting

Experiments have been executed on a corpus extracted from DBpedia about 101 well known computer scientists, described by the following features:

The total number of LOD resources included in the corpus is 404 and the total number of triples is 518. Moreover, the corpus contains also 1055 LOD types.

Feature	# of values	% of unique values
almaMater	88	57 %
award	102	52 %
birthPlace	105	81 %
deathPlace	48	88 %
doctoralAdvisor	23	87 %
field	76	29 %
influenced	27	100 %
influencedBy	6	100 %
nationality	27	33 %
residence	16	38 %

Ground-Truth Definition. We asked a group of database experts to analyze the LOD corpus in order to manually create two cluster sets. In performing this activity, the experts directly queried DBpedia through a SPARQL endpoint. For the creation of the first cluster set, we asked the experts to group LOD resources by following a criterion based on the professional information available about computer scientists and by focusing on the features included in the professional dimension $\mathcal{D}_{pro}$, which is composed by the features {almaMater, award, doctoralAdvisor, field, influenced, influencedBy}. For the creation of the second cluster set, we asked the experts to focus on the geographic dimension $\mathcal{D}_{geo}$, which is composed by the features {birthPlace, deathPlace, nationality, residence}. In the remaining of this section we will refer to the manually created cluster sets as *category sets* (and the clusters therein contained as *categories*) and they will be denoted as $L^{\mathcal{D}_{pro}}$ and $L^{\mathcal{D}_{geo}}$, respectively. The category sets are used in the evaluation as a ground-truth to rely on for comparison against single-dimension and multi-dimension cluster sets.

Evaluation Measures. For evaluation, we use three well-known measures for clustering comparison, namely *Purity* [26], *F-measure* [20] and the *Rand coefficient* [11]. Purity is a measure based on the frequency of the correspondence between the most common category and each cluster [1]. Given C as the cluster set under evaluation, L as the category set, and N the number of clustered resources, purity is defined as follows:

$$Purity(L, C) = \sum_i \frac{|C_i|}{N} max_j\{Precision(L_j, C_i)\}$$

where precision is defined as:

$$Precision(L_j, C_i) = \frac{|L_j \cap C_i|}{|C_i|}$$

Purity is basically a redesign of the classical Information Retrieval precision for the purpose of cluster sets comparison. Thus, purity measures the level of correspondence between a cluster set generated by HC^{f+} and the category set manually defined.

F-measure complements purity in that it takes into account not only the precision of cluster sets but also their recall, namely the capability of a cluster set to cover all the categories in the category set. F-measure is defined as follows:

$$F = \sum_i \frac{|L_i|}{N} max_j \{F(L_i, C_j)\}$$

where:

$$F(L_i, C_j) = \frac{2 \cdot Recall(L_i, C_j) \cdot Precision(L_i, C_j)}{Recall(L_i, C_j) + Precision(L_i, C_j)}$$

$$Recall(L_i, C_j) = \frac{|L_i \cap C_j|}{|L_i|}$$

Finally, the Rand coefficient is based on a different approach to the evaluation of cluster sets quality. The idea is to analyze pairs of resources and their placement in clusters and categories. In particular, we calculate four statistics: (i) TT, the number of resource pairs appearing in the same category and cluster; (ii) TF, the number of resource pairs appearing in the same category but different cluster; (iii) FT, the number of resource pairs appearing in the same cluster but different category; (iv) FF, the number of resource pairs appearing in different cluster and category [1]. In other words, $TT + FF$ is the number of resources that have been clustered consistently in a category as well as in a cluster set, while $TF + FT$ is the number of resources that have been clustered differently in the category and the cluster set. According to these statistics, the Rand coefficient is calculated as the total number of consistent results over the total number of resource pairs:

$$Rand(L_j, C_i) = \frac{TT + FF}{TT + TF + FT + FF}$$

In our evaluation, the Rand coefficient is used to check the robustness of the results of purity and to provide a more analytical measure of correspondence, based on individual resource pairs and their placement in the cluster sets.

8.2   Dimensional Data Clustering

In this evaluation, we analyze the results of single-dimension clustering with respect to the results of classical hierarchical clustering. Two different tests are executed. In the first test, the category set $L^{\mathcal{D}_{pro}}$ of the ground truth is compared against (i) $CL^{\mathcal{D}_{pro}}$, that is the cluster set obtained through dimensional clustering over the $\mathcal{D}_{pro}$ dimension, and (ii) H, that is the cluster set obtained through the classical hierarchical clustering with the complete-link strategy. Similarly, in the second test, the category set $L^{\mathcal{D}_{geo}}$ of the ground truth is compared against $CL^{\mathcal{D}_{geo}}$ and H. For each comparison between cluster sets and categories, purity, F-measure and Rand coefficient have been calculated.

Purity. Purity evaluation results are shown in Fig. 10. We note that both the professional dimension $\mathcal{D}_{pro}$ and the geographic dimension $CL^{\mathcal{D}_{geo}}$ generated by our dimensional clustering provide better results than the hierarchical algorithm H. Moreover, we note that the results of the geographic dimension are better than the professional dimension. This is due to the fact that the professional dimension contains the feature field, which has a low number of unique values in the corpus. This produces many similarity values due to the field feature which is not a discriminating feature for the considered resources. For this reason, the classical hierarchical clustering algorithm H, which does not discriminate the causes of similarity, has a behavior quite similar to our dimensional approach. Results are better for $CL^{\mathcal{D}_{geo}}$, where such non-discriminating similarity values over the professional dimension are not considered in clustering. For this reason, the purity of $CL^{\mathcal{D}_{geo}}$ is significantly higher than the hierarchical clustering H.

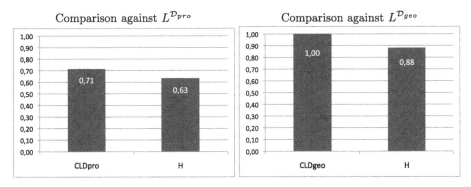

Fig. 10. Purity evaluation results

F-Measure. F-measure evaluation results are shown in Fig. 11. The F-measure results confirm purity results for both the professional and the geographic dimensions. This means that the dimensional clustering provides a better coverage of the categories manually defined than the classical hierarchical clustering. As for purity, we observe that the presence of a non-discriminating feature like field downgrades the quality of both $CL^{\mathcal{D}_{pro}}$ and H.

Rand Coefficient. Rand evaluation results are shown in Fig. 12. As for purity and F-measure, the Rand coefficient confirms that dimensional clustering performs better than hierarchical clustering for both $\mathcal{D}_{pro}$ and $\mathcal{D}_{geo}$ dimensions. However, we observe that the results over the professional dimension are quite

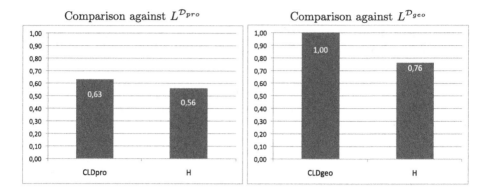

Fig. 11. F-measure evaluation results

poor for both $CL^{\mathcal{D}_{pro}}$ and H. This means that the expected results of the category set $L^{\mathcal{D}_{pro}}$, and thus of the experts that manually defined $L^{\mathcal{D}_{pro}}$, is not compliant with the two clustering algorithms, regardless their peculiar characteristics. On the opposite, the results over the geographic dimension are excellent for both $CL^{\mathcal{D}_{geo}}$ and H, meaning that the two algorithms succeed in providing the expected results of $L^{\mathcal{D}_{geo}}$.

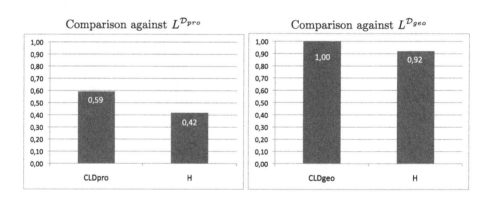

Fig. 12. Rand coefficient evaluation results

8.3   Evaluation of Cluster Ensemble

In this evaluation, we compare the multi-dimension cluster sets obtained through ensemble of $CL^{\mathcal{D}_{pro}}$ and $CL^{\mathcal{D}_{geo}}$ against the cluster set $\mathsf{ALL} = CL^{\mathcal{D}_{pro} \cup \mathcal{D}_{geo}}$ obtained through a single execution of matching and clustering over all the features in $\mathcal{D}_{pro} \cup \mathcal{D}_{geo}$ (that we call *flat clustering*).

Ensemble Comparison. For this evaluation, we apply ensemble techniques over $CL^{\mathcal{D}_{pro}}$ and $CL^{\mathcal{D}_{geo}}$ by executing all the possible operations, criteria, and modalities described in Sect. 6. As a result, we generate 12 cluster sets, each one associated with a label describing the applied operation ('I' for intersection, 'U' for union, 'D' for difference), criterion ('C' for centrality-driven and 'M' for mutuality-driven), and policy ('O' for one-to-one and 'M' for one-to-many). For example, the cluster set ICO is obtained by applying the intersection operation, the centrality-driven criterion, and the one-to-one policy.

The 12 cluster sets obtained through ensemble and the ALL cluster set are compared against the category sets $L^{\mathcal{D}_{pro}}$ and $L^{\mathcal{D}_{geo}}$ by using purity, F-measure, and Rand coefficient. The results of this comparison are shown in Fig. 13. For what concerns purity, the ensemble approach is better than the flat clustering in all the considered situations, regardless the adopted operation, criterion, and policy. For that concerns F-measure and Rand coefficient, the results of ensemble and flat clustering are comparable, however, we note that ensemble outperforms flat clustering in some situations. As a general remark, we note that the union operation provides better results with respect to F-measure, while intersection operation provides better results with respect to the Rand coefficient. This is due to the fact that the union operation produces large clusters that have more probability to cover the expected category set. On the opposite, the intersection operation produces small clusters where resources are strictly coupled and, thus, the probability to meet the expected result of the category set manually produced by experts is high.

Ensemble Analysis. In order to better understand the ensemble results, we execute a more analytic comparison between the cluster set ALL and the cluster set IMM obtained through ensemble with intersection operation, mutuality-driven criterion, and one-to-many policy. The IMM cluster set has been chosen since it provides the best performance on average for purity, F-measure, and Rand coefficient in both the category sets $L^{\mathcal{D}_{pro}}$ and $L^{\mathcal{D}_{geo}}$. Consider a cluster $cl_i \in$ ALL $\cup$ IMM and the associated feature set πcl_i that generated the cluster cl_i in the execution of the HC^{f+} algorithm. We are interested in measuring how much the cluster cl_i is professional and/or geographical oriented. To this end, for a cluster cl_i, we calculate the professional coefficient p_i and the geographic coefficient g_i as follows:

$$p_i = \frac{\mid \pi cl_i \cap \mathcal{D}_{pro} \mid}{\mid \pi cl_i \mid}, \; g_i = \frac{\mid \pi cl_i \cap \mathcal{D}_{geo} \mid}{\mid \pi cl_i \mid}$$

For each cluster $cl_i \in$ ALL $\cup$ IMM, the corresponding professional p_i and geographic g_i coefficients are represented on the scatter plot of Fig. 14. The distribution of clusters along the professional and geographic dimensions show that the ALL cluster set is mainly composed by mixed clusters, where the causes of similarity are combined by professional and geographic features, except for a very small number of clusters that contain resources mainly focused on professional features (right-bottom side of the scatter plot). Instead, most of the clusters

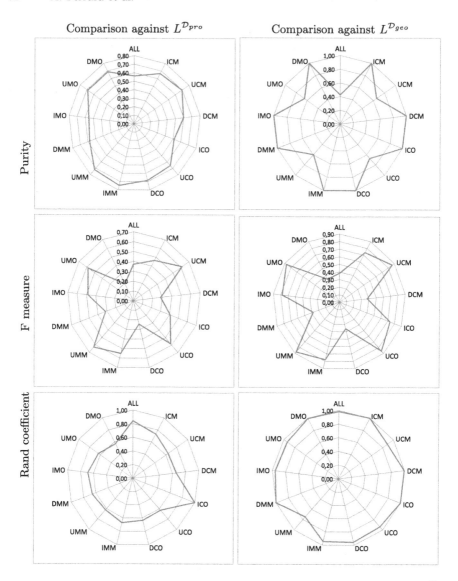

Fig. 13. Comparison of ensemble and ALL cluster sets against the category sets $L^{\mathcal{D}_{pro}}$ and $L^{\mathcal{D}_{geo}}$

belonging to the IMM cluster set are balanced on professional and geographic dimensions (central part of the scatter plot). A certain number of clusters where one of the two dimensions (e.g., professional) is prevalent are also preserved (right-middle side of the scatter plot). We can conclude that both cluster sets succeed in preserving clusters that are mixed on the two dimensions. The IMM cluster set outperforms the ALL cluster set in preserving clusters where one dimension is prevailing on the other one.

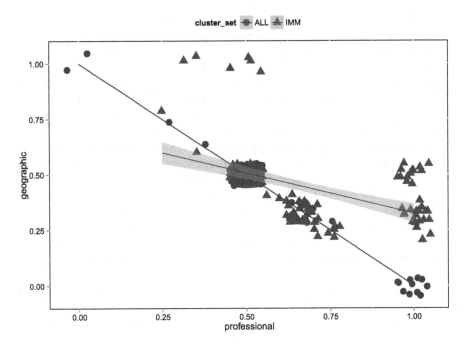

Fig. 14. Analysis of ALL and IMM cluster sets

9   Related Work

Work related to dimensional clustering is in the field of linked data matching, data clustering, and cluster ensemble.

Linked data matching is emerging in the recent years and a number of approaches and tools are being appearing [12,24]. Here, we focus on the problem of optimizing the matching process by reducing the number of comparisons to perform. According to the survey in [7], our matching techniques presented in Sect. 4 belong to the field of value-oriented techniques and rely on methods for the reduction of the comparison costs based on feature selection. Similar techniques are presented in [23] where a pre-matching phase is applied to find the comparison classes in a given comparison space. In [23], to reduce the number of matching comparisons, a standard text-normalization process is executed (e.g., converting the textual values in lower case, removing special characters, converting all the numeric values to a common measure unit) and data values are reduced according to a prefixed number of categories (e.g., "Rob", "Robert" and "Robbie", in the field "Name", are all represented by "Robert"). With respect to the approach of [23], our matching techniques rely on dimensions to discriminate between comparable and non-comparable features without any pre-processing activity.

About data clustering, the dimension-based clustering techniques presented in Sect. 5 can be defined as agglomerative and hierarchical according to the survey classification of clustering algorithm proposed in [3]. In this paper, we focus on issues about the quality of the cluster sets resulting from dimension-based application of the clustering algorithm [1,19]. In this respect, an interesting work is [14] where a two-phase clustering procedure is presented. In a former step, a feature set is extracted for each document and aggregated to obtain a collection of feature sets. In a latter step, these feature sets are used as input for a soft clustering algorithm. This approach is based on the use of features as aggregation criterion and the items of a cluster can have different sets of common features as a result. With respect to this solution, our HC^{f+} algorithm presents two main differences. First, HC^{f+} is driven by the comprehensive similarity values among items instead of relying on specific similarity values among features. Second, HC^{f+} produces clusters with associated similarity features that are common to all the cluster members. This means that clusters are cohesive with respect to features. Similarly to HC^{f+}, an approach focused on obtaining clusters with homogeneous feature values is proposed in [27]. As a difference with such a solution, HC^{f+} is focused only on feature similarity and it also supports cluster overlaps.

Dimensional clustering is also concerned with cluster ensemble [22]. In this field, techniques are used in two main contexts: knowledge reuse (e.g., for distributed-computing purposes) and cluster-accuracy improvement. For knowledge reuse, the cluster ensemble is employed to merge the results of partial clustering executions applied to subsamples of the available data. This allows a parallelization of the clustering phase leading to a reduced execution time. In both [21] and [15], an approach is proposed where the original dataset is divided into multiple subsamples and the clustering results are finally merged relying on different cluster ensemble techniques. In [21], the cluster ensemble technique is based on a notion of mutual information between clusters to choose the candidates for merging. In [15], a consensus-based technique is proposed, where the partial clusterings are used to compute new similarity values between the resources. The main idea of [15] is that the higher is the number of clusterings where two resources appear in the same cluster, the higher will be the similarity between these two resources. About [15], a number of techniques has been proposed to select the cluster candidates for merging, by relying on mutual information [19], best-match finding, interaction probability and cluster reduction techniques [10]. For cluster-accuracy improvement, multiple clustering solutions are computed (e.g., for different data representations) and ensemble techniques are finally applied to obtain an overall clustering result. In [16], different approaches for computing multiple clustering solutions are analyzed while in [2] the focus is on obtaining a high-quality cluster set maximizing the dissimilarity with a given previously-computed clustering. The goal is to consider all the different aspects of the analyzed data. A similar approach is presented in [13], where a further step is performed by proposing two different techniques for cluster merging. With respect to the above approaches, we propose to use ensemble techniques as a tool, enabling the user to effectively explore a (possibly) large corpus of linked data. The generation of multiple dimension-based cluster sets is enforced to support different views of the same corpus and ensemble operations and related techniques are provided to enable the "on-the-fly" combination of these views according to the specific user preferences.

10 Concluding Remarks

In this paper, we presented techniques for dimensional clustering of linked data based on thematic dimensions. In particular, we focused on techniques for (i) the creation of a single-dimension cluster set through matching and clustering, and (ii) the generation of a multi-dimension cluster set through clustering ensemble. Single- and multi-dimension cluster sets are used to support effective exploration of a given corpus of linked data under different and complementary thematic perspectives.

Ongoing activities are about the development of a suite of prototype tools implementing the various techniques presented in this paper for dimensional data clustering and cluster ensemble. Future activities will be devoted to integrate these prototype tools with the summarization and exploration mechanisms outlined in Sect. 7.

References

1. Amigó, E., Gonzalo, J., Artiles, J., Verdejo, F.: A comparison of extrinsic clustering evaluation metrics based on formal constraints. Inf. Retr. **12**(4), 461–486 (2009)
2. Bae, E., Bailey, J.: COALA: a novel approach for the extraction of an alternate clustering of high quality and high dissimilarity. In: Proceedings of the 6th IEEE International Conference on Data Mining (ICDM 2006), Hong Kong, China, pp. 53–62 (2006)
3. Berkhin, P.: A survey of clustering data mining techniques. In: Kogan, J., Nicholas, C., Teboulle, M. (eds.) Grouping Multidimensional Data. Springer, Heidelberg (2006)
4. Bizer, C., Heath, T., Berners-Lee, T.: Linked data - the story so far. Int. J. Semant. Web Inf. Syst. **5**(3), 1–22 (2009)
5. Castano, S., Ferrara, A., Montanelli, S.: Thematic clustering and exploration of linked data. In: Ceri, S., Brambilla, M. (eds.) Search Computing. LNCS, vol. 7538, pp. 157–175. Springer, Heidelberg (2012)
6. Drost, I., Bickel, S., Scheffer, T.: Discovering communities in linked data by multi-view clustering. In: Proceedings of the 29th Annual Conference of the Gesellschaft für Klassifikation, Magdeburg, Germany, pp. 342–349 (2005)
7. Ferrara, A., Nikolov, A., Scharffe, F.: Data linking for the semantic web. Int. J. Semant. Web Inf. Syst. **7**(3), 46–76 (2011)
8. Ferrara, A., Genta, L., Montanelli, S.: Linked data classification: a feature-based approach. In: Proceedings of the 3rd EDBT International Workshop on Linked Web Data Management (LWDM 2013), Genova, Italy (2013)
9. Giannakidou, E., Vakali, A.: Integrating web 2.0 data into linked open data cloud via clustering. In: Proceedings of the Workshop on Linked Data in the Future Internet at the Future Internet Assembly, Ghent, Belgium (2010)

10. Goldberg, M.K., Hayvanovych, M., Magdon-Ismail, M.: Measuring similarity between sets of overlapping clusters. In: Proceedings of the IEEE Social-Com/PASSAT Conference, Minneapolis, Minnesota, USA, pp. 303–308 (2010)

11. Halkidi, M., Batistakis, Y., Vazirgiannis, M.: On clustering validation techniques. J. Intell. Inf. Syst. **17**(2–3), 107–145 (2001)

12. Jean-Mary, Y.R., Shironoshita, E.P., Kabuka, M.R.: Ontology matching with semantic verification. J. Web Semant. **7**(3), 235–251 (2009)

13. Kailing, K., Kriegel, H.-P., Pryakhin, A., Schubert, M.: Clustering multi-represented objects with noise. In: Dai, H., Srikant, R., Zhang, C. (eds.) PAKDD 2004. LNCS (LNAI), vol. 3056, pp. 394–403. Springer, Heidelberg (2004)

14. Lu, Q., Conrad, J.G., Al-Kofahi, K., Keenan, W.: Legal document clustering with built-in topic segmentation. In: Proceedings of the 20th ACM Conference on Information and Knowledge Management (CIKM 2011), Glasgow, UK (2011)

15. Minaei-Bidgoli, B., Topchy, A.P., Punch, W.F.: A comparison of resampling methods for clustering ensembles. In: Proceedings of the International Conference on Artificial Intelligence (IC-AI 2004), Las Vegas, Nevada, USA, pp. 939–945 (2004)

16. Müller, E., Günnemann, S., Färber, I., Seidl, T.: Discovering multiple clustering solutions: grouping objects in different views of the data. In: Proceedings of the 28th IEEE International Conference on Data Engineering (ICDE 2012), Washington, DC, USA, pp. 1207–1210 (2012)

17. Navarro, G.: A guided tour to approximate string matching. ACM Comput. Surv. **33**(1), 31–88 (2001)

18. Newman, M.J.: A measure of betweenness centrality based on random walks. Soc. Netw. **27**(1), 39–54 (2005)

19. Nguyen, X.V., Epps, J., Bailey, J.: Information theoretic measures for clusterings comparison: is a correction for chance necessary? In: Proceedings of the 26th Annual International Conference on Machine Learning (ICML 2009), Montreal, Quebec, Canada (2009)

20. Steinbach, M., Karypis, G., Kumar, V., et al.: A comparison of document clustering techniques. In: Proceedings of the 6th ACM SIGKDD KDD-2000 Workshop on Text Mining, Boston, MA, USA (2000)

21. Strehl, A., Ghosh, J.: Cluster ensembles – a knowledge reuse framework for combining multiple partitions. J. Mach. Learn. Res. **3**, 583–617 (2002)

22. Vega-Pons, S., Ruiz-Shulcloper, J.: A survey of clustering ensemble algorithms. Int. J. Pattern Recogn. Artif. Intell. **25**(3), 337–372 (2011)

23. Verykios, V.S., Elmagarmid, A.K., Houstis, E.N.: Automating the approximate record-matching process. Inf. Sci. **126**(1–4), 83–98 (2000)

24. Wang, Z., Li, J., Zhao, Y., Setchi, R., Tang, J.: A unified approach to matching semantic data on the web. Knowl. Based Syst. **39**, 173–184 (2013)

25. Xu, R., Wunsch II, D.C.: Survey of clustering algorithms. IEEE Trans. Neural Netw. **16**(3), 645–678 (2005)

26. Zhao, Y., Karypis, G.: Empirical and theoretical comparisons of selected criterion functions for document clustering. Mach. Learn. **55**(3), 311–331 (2004)

27. Zhou, Y., Cheng, H., Yu, J.X.: Graph clustering based on structural/attribute similarities. Proc. VLDB Endow. **2**(1), 718–729 (2009)

ProProtect3: An Approach for Protecting User Profile Data from Disclosure, Tampering, and Improper Use in the Context of WebID

Stefan Wild[✉], Fabian Wiedemann, Sebastian Heil, Alexey Tschudnowsky, and Martin Gaedke

Technische Universität Chemnitz, Chemnitz, Germany
{Stefan.Wild,Fabian.Wiedemann,Sebastian.Heil,
Alexey.Tschudnowsky,Martin.Gaedke}@informatik.tu-chemnitz.de

Abstract. WebID is a new identification approach of the W3C. It enables managing profile data associated to persons and services at self-defined places in the cloud. By relying on RDF vocabularies like FOAF for describing user profile data, WebID contributes to the Semantic Web vision. While access to user profiles can be controlled with existing security mechanisms, they are not designed to protect sensitive data *within* user profiles from unwanted retrieval, malicious manipulation, and improper use. This article analyzes the risks that affect the knowledge stored in WebID-based user profiles. It therefore describes potential attack scenarios and outlines the challenges a solution must deal with. To tackle the problem of insufficient protection, we propose ProProtect3. This approach enables identity owners (1) to create customized filters for sensitive data, (2) to verify the profile data integrity, and (3) to restrict the rights of delegatees. For evaluating the ProProtect3 approach, we integrate it into a WebID identity provider.

Keywords: Protection · Linked data · Identity · WebID · Social web · Privacy · Security · Integrity · Authentication · Delegation · Semantic web

1 Introduction

With increasing presence of social media in daily activities, the need for trustworthy collaboration is becoming more and more important [14,35]. Centralized social networks like Facebook, Google+ or LinkedIn provide varied possibilities for personal information exchange and networking, but try to lock-in users within social network domains [45]. As recent security disclosures have shown, such walled gardens allow for large scale analysis of user data [17]. Some of the involved companies, e.g., Google, Yahoo! or Microsoft, also act as identity providers. They offer single sign-on functionality for avoiding problems summarized by the term *password fatigue* [24]. Although a growing number of social networks tends to make parts of their collected knowledge available to the public through APIs [31], users are not in full control of their identity data. Preventing

© Springer-Verlag Berlin Heidelberg 2015
A. Hameurlain et al. (Eds.): TLDKS XIX, LNCS 8990, pp. 87–127, 2015.
DOI: 10.1007/978-3-662-46562-2_4

the creation of data silos and enabling users to remain in control of their personal data asks for a distributed online social network [45].

A distributed online social network can be implemented on the basis of W3C's WebID specification [38]. WebID represents a distributed identification approach enabling users to globally authenticate themselves, connect to each other and manage their identity data at a self-defined place [34]. The WebID approach makes use of three important artifacts: the WebID URI, the WebID profile, and the WebID certificate. These artifacts are shown in Fig. 1 and described below.

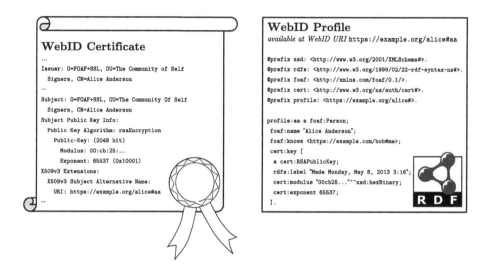

Fig. 1. Artifacts in WebID: Certificate, URI, and Profile

A **WebID URI** refers to an identity $i \in I$, where I is the set of all identities and i typically is a person, but it can also be a robot or a group, or more generally spoken an agent. Like a username in other identity systems, a WebID URI $w \in W \subset U$ is a URI denoting an identity i, where W is the set of all WebID URIs and U the set of all URIs. Dereferencing a WebID URI w returns a set of RDF triples $T \in \mathfrak{T}$ that describe personal attributes of identity i using Linked Data, where $\mathfrak{T}$ is the set of all RDF triples. This is formalized in Eq. (1). There, function $d(u)$ yields T for URI u being a valid WebID URI.

$$W = \{u | d(u) = T\}, u \in U \tag{1}$$

A **WebID profile** is a URI addressable resource, which is available at WebID URI w and contains a set of RDF triples T describing identity i. Each triple $t \in T$ consists of subject t_1, predicate t_2, and object t_3. As RDF is used for specifying all personal data, an identity's attributes are expressive, extensible and machine-readable [28]. This is a major advantages to other identity systems, which are restricted in assigning and exchanging user attributes. Such semantic profile descriptions facilitate large scale exploitation of profile data to optimize customer services and improve the user experience [42]. While RDF allows for using various ontologies, a WebID profile primarily relies on FOAF as a vocabulary for personal data [6]. As a set of RDF triples T spans graph $G = (V, E), G \in \mathfrak{G}$, where $\mathfrak{G}$ is the set of all graphs, and graph G describes a set of triples describing identity i, we formalize this equivalence in Eq. (2).

$$T \sim G \Leftrightarrow \forall t = (t_1, t_2, t_3) \in T : t_1, t_2, t_3 \in V \wedge (t_1, t_2) \in E \wedge (t_2, t_3) \in E \quad (2)$$

Besides being a semantic repository for personal data, a WebID profile also contains a set of public keys described by triples $T_P \subset T$. Each single public key $k \in K$ is described by triples $T_k \subseteq T_P$, where $K \subset \mathfrak{K}$ is the set of asymmetric keys owned by identity i and $\mathfrak{K}$ the set of all asymmetric keys. T_k specifies diverse attributes of a public key k, including type, modulus and exponent. A k-corresponding private key $k^{-1} \in K$ is used to prove that an identity actually owns the public key k. Equation (3) defines the relation between k and k^{-1} using function a, which maps messages M and the set of keys $\mathfrak{K}$ on the set of messages.

$$a : \mathfrak{K} \times M \rightarrow M \qquad a(k, a(k^{-1}, m)) = m \quad \forall m \in M \quad (3)$$

A **WebID certificate** is an X.509 client certificate [9]. As formalized by Eq. (4), a WebID certificate $C_{i,k} \in C_i$ contains the WebID URI w of identity i and a public key k owned by identity i, where C_i is the set of all WebID certificates of i. Here, the *Subject Alternative Name* property of the certificate stores w. WebID certificate $C_{i,k}$ is signed with the corresponding private key k^{-1} or the private key of a trusted party.

$$C_{i,k} = (w, k) \quad (4)$$

An identity $i = (w, T)$ is described by a WebID URI w and personal data T contained in the associated WebID profile. Unlike knowledge-based authentication approaches using username/password pairs as proof of identity, WebID is an ownership-based authentication approach. For authentication, it relies on public key data available in both WebID profile and certificate. An identity i is authenticatable when i has a WebID certificate $C_{i,k}$ containing a public key k for which i owns the corresponding private key k^{-1}, as defined in Eq. (5).

$$i = (w, T) \text{ is authenticatable} \Leftrightarrow \exists k : T_k \subset T, \exists C_{i,k}, \exists k^{-1} \quad (5)$$

This part of the authentication is performed after the ownership of the private key k^{-1} is proven during the TLS handshake [11].

Figure 2 illustrates the process[1] of retrieving a resource from a server that allows users to authenticate via WebID. This process shows how the previously described WebID artifacts are used. There, a subject, called Alice, requests a particular resource stored on the server. Having established a TLS-secured connection in ①, Alice's actual request sent in ② is directly intercepted by a guard

---

[1] The sequence diagram is based on the WebID authentication sequence (cf. [34]).

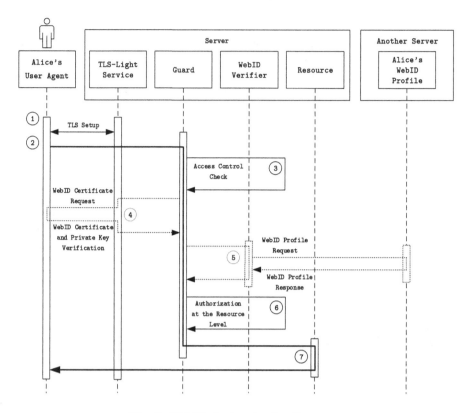

Fig. 2. WebID Authentication Sequence

shielding the server. The guard parses the request to detect access control settings associated to the request target in ③. If the requested resource is access controlled, Alice is asked to authenticate by providing a WebID certificate in ④. Given that Alice selected a WebID certificate to which she has the private key, the public key of the certificate is compared to a valid one found in Alice's WebID profile. The WebID verifier, being responsible for this check, automatically retrieves Alice's WebID profile by dereferencing the WebID URI stored in WebID certificate provided by Alice. Here, the WebID profile is hosted on another server. Assuming that both public keys are identified as equal in ⑤, Alice is potentially granted access to the requested resource in ⑥, which she retrieves in ⑦.

Alice's WebID profile has been retrieved during authentication for verifying her proof of identity. Her profile has to be accessible to do so. The verification routine processes her profile unaware of the integrity and the correctness of data stored within. While today's security mechanisms are designed to protect resources against risks that originate from outside (cf. ③ and ⑥), they lack providing adequate protection from threats that emerge from inside.

In WebID, every user is enabled self-host an identity provider and self-assign arbitrary identity data. So, special attention needs to be paid to protect the systems that host the user profile data. No other identity approach is known to the authors that allows for using identity data in such an expressive, extensible and machine-readable way. With only a small extent of user profile data available to be disclosed, other approaches do not necessarily require sophisticated protection means. Centralized identity approaches can rely on some trained personnel to protect a few *central* systems that host the user profiles.

1.1   Problem of Insufficiently Protected User Profile Data

An insufficiently protected WebID profile is a potential source of information for subjects that collect, tamper, or improperly use user profile data. There are different manifestations of this problem that affect the identity owner's privacy and reputation. They are outlined below.

Information stored within a WebID profile can be retrieved by known and wanted, but also unknown and unwanted subjects. Since WebID profiles are parsed during authentication to verify public key data, they must be accessible for other services and agents. That is, also profile data irrelevant to the authentication procedure per se could be retrieved and collected without the identity owner's notice. So, data found within WebID profiles could be used for purposes identity owners do not agree with, e.g., product marketing or social network analysis.

While data-collecting subjects can be considered as attackers from the outside, a WebID profile could be also attacked from the inside. Malicious administrators could tamper data stored within the profile when hosted on a non-trustworthy server. Purposeful manipulation of WebID profile data enables defamation, e.g., by adding a wanted criminal as a social connection. Beyond that, it even facilitates identity theft, e.g., by adding the identity thief's public key to the WebID profile.

Above problem manifestations can happen without the identity owner's intent or knowledge. There is, however, another one which can take effect on the identity owner's initiative. In a delegation scenario, the identity owner authorizes somebody to do something on her behalf. This *something* needs to be precisely specified and enforced by appropriate measures. Otherwise, delegatees could improperly use this authorization to do unspecified things in the identity owner's name.

1.2   Contributions for an Improved Protection of User Profile Data

To deal with the problem of insufficiently protected user profiles, we aim at enabling identity owners to protect their WebID profile data from unwanted retrieval, tampering, and improper use. Addressing all problem manifestations, we propose the ProProtect3 approach that contributes achieving the following objectives:

1. To avoid unwanted retrieval of sensitive user profile data.
2. To detect malicious manipulations in WebID profiles.
3. To prevent improper use of profile data by delegatees.

Even though WebID is still in development and has not reached a critical user acceptance so far, not dealing with the problem will impede further adoption and progress. We expect that solving the problem with ProProtect3 will contribute to increase the user acceptance of WebID. The more secure a user identity is considered to be, the more users WebID will gain. Allowing users to protect their profiles as personal knowledge bases will add to advance the overall information security in the context of knowledge centered systems and Linked Data.

Although there are other factors that affect the security in the WebID context, this article's scope is limited to the protection of data stored *within* WebID profiles. One of these other factors is the procedure used for creating WebID certificates from within browsers. There, users risk to make wrong decisions, which impair their privacy and security. We discuss this issue in [41].

The rest of the article is organized as follows: Sect. 2 describes scenarios to highlight diverse problem facets. Section 3 derives the challenges from these scenarios a solution must deal with. Section 4 presents the ProProtect3 approach. We explain how this threefold approach achieves protection against unwanted retrieval in Sect. 5, against malicious manipulation in Sect. 6, and against improper use in Sect. 7. Section 8 evaluates the approach based on a prototypical implementation in the Sociddea WebID identity provider. Section 9 discusses related work. Section 10 concludes the article and points to future work.

2   Scenarios Indicating Insufficient Profile Protection

For highlighting the problem of insufficiently protected user profile data in the context of WebID, we use different characters that pursue different goals:

Alice is a WebID identity owner. She intends to protect her profile against various threats. However, Alice does not want to make too many efforts to achieve this goal. Although Alice has basic IT knowledge, she is not that experienced. At work, Alice acts as a delegator, i.e., a person who can delegate tasks to co-workers.

Bob is a close friend to Alice. Alice trusts him and Bob trusts her. Bob is allowed to see private data contained within her WebID profile.

Casey is another friend of Alice. Compared to Bob, he is not that close to Alice. For instance, Casey could be a co-worker of her. While Alice trusts Casey in work-related activities, she does not share any private data stored within her profile with him. Since Alice also acts as a delegator at work, she can hand over tasks to him. Here Casey is a delegatee, i.e., a person who is assigned to a task.

Dave is another friend of Alice having Casey's characteristics.

Mallory is the bad guy; Alice's enemy. He is the malicious attacker who actively wants to impair or damage Alice's identity and associated data contained within her WebID profile. Mallory can be considered as the opposite of Bob with regard to Alice. He intends to attack her user profile data at all costs. Mallory acts as a malicious server operator.

Having described the personae that are used throughout this article, we explain risk factors and attack scenarios next. They illustrate several aspects of the problem of insufficiently protected user profile data in the WebID context.

Scenario 1. As a WebID identity owner, Alice intends to restrict her profile data's visibility. She wants to do this because all information available inside her WebID profile could be easily retrieved, if not properly addressed by appropriate access control mechanisms. Sensitive profile data could be used for purposes she does not agree with, e.g., social network analysis, tailored advertisements or product marketing. Although restricting access to her entire profile would be an option, Alice is not interested in losing advantages like authentication or single-sign-on to new yet unknown services. To keep associated services up-to-date, Alice wants to permit monitoring specific profile parts by third-party entities for changes. Alice wants to allow anyone to access profile data she marked as visible, even if Alice is currently unavailable or unauthenticated.

Scenario 2. Bob wants to retrieve Alice's current address data. As Alice knows and trusts Bob, she granted him more visibility rights compared to the anonymous subjects in Scenario 1. While Bob is allowed to see Alice's private address data, Alice does not want to share this kind of data with her co-worker Casey. Instead of private address data, only Alice's office address data is visible to Casey.

Scenario 3. Alice's WebID profile is hosted on a server she trusted in the past. Today, she does not trust the server operator any longer. Therefore, Alice plans to switch the server hosting her WebID profile. Alice has distributed her WebID profile data to separate resources for applying access rights at the resource level. For migrating to a new hosting server, Alice has to find, consolidate, and transfer all her user profile data being scattered among various resources. Additionally, she has to adjust access control lists (ACLs) for these resources due to different hosting locations, naming restrictions etc. As an identity owner, Alice must be aware of all resources relevant to the migration. Depending on Alices setup used for securing her personal data, this migration might be a complex undertaking.

Scenario 4. Alice's WebID profile is hosted on a server operated by Mallory. She controls access to her WebID profile at the resource level to avoid data disclosure from the outside (cf. Scenarios 1 and 3). However, she cannot apply the same access control for the inside. When hosting her profile there, Alice was aware of the risk that Mallory could disclose all her profile data[2]. Apart from this fact, Mallory can also manipulate Alice's WebID profile data. As an example, he would be enabled to change her email address to point to one of his own or add new social connections linking to wanted criminals or Alice's enemies. That is, Mallory can tamper Alice's user profile data without her knowledge and notice.

Scenario 5. Based on Scenario 4, Mallory wants to take full control of Alice's WebID profile. For this purpose, he adds his own public key to Alice's profile. Mallory creates a WebID certificate linking to her profile. That is, Mallory's WebID certificate contains the public key that is also available in Alice's WebID profile. As a consequence, Mallory is enabled to authenticate himself using Alice's

---

[2] This common risk affects all unencrypted files hosted on third party operated servers.

identity. To make this even worse, he removes all other public keys from her WebID profile. Thus, Alice cannot authenticate herself to other subjects any longer. She has to inform all her social connections and services accessing her profile about the forgery. Finally, she has to choose a new WebID URI and re-create both her certificates and her profile.

Scenario 6. Mallory permanently tampered Alice's user profile data in Scenarios 4 and 5. Alice might find out about such malicious manipulations sooner or later. To cover his tracks, Mallory adjusted his approach and only tampers her WebID profile data on special occasions, now. That is, his modifications to Alice's profile are temporary instead of permanently. As an example, before authenticating to a service as Alice, Mallory adds his public key to her WebID profile (cf. Scenario 5). After making use of these services as Alice, Mallory reverses his malicious changes by removing his public key. In the time between these events, Mallory could send emails, book or order something in her name. In this case, Alice probably will not discover that a malicious manipulation of her profile data was the reason for future events and issues.

Scenario 7. As Alice is a busy person, she delegates tasks to other persons to act on her behalf. These persons should have access to her WebID profile data for using it to accomplish the task in her name. She knows that her authorization would not be misused for other purposes, when she is delegating a task to a person she fully trusts. While this is the case with Bob, Alice is not sure regarding Casey as delegatee. When Casey uses Alice's authorization intentionally, he usually acts on her behalf within her specified scope, but sometimes he also does other things in her name. This is an improper use of her authorization. Alice therefore wants to be aware of Casey activities that are done on her behalf.

Scenario 8. In addition to Scenario 7, Casey has to work on Alice's behalf on a task having a fixed deadline, e.g., a project proposal. Alice does not want Casey to work on that task on her behalf outside the specified time frame. She tries to prevent Casey from misusing her authorization for other things. Unlike Casey, Dave works in Alice's name on a regular basis, e.g., for creating status report.

Scenario 9. In addition to Scenario 7, Alice delegates a task to Casey that involves using a specific service, like a travel booking portal, on her behalf. Alice does not want Casey to use other unspecified services in her name.

The scenarios describe potential risks and attacks. They deal with different issues related to data stored in user profiles. We analyze them in the next section.

3   Analysis of Protection Needs

In this section, we discuss the findings gained from analyzing the scenarios described in Sect. 2. We extract protection needs of identity owners and outline that applying today's approaches cannot solve these issues completely. It is furthermore shown that there is a research gap we try to close in this article.

Scenario 1 shows a need that identity owners want to restrict access to sensitive data within their profiles. They want to do this without impairing the features introduced with WebID, e.g., certificate-based authentication and personal data repositories. To allow monitoring by services an identity owner uses, WebID profiles must remain accessible. This general protection is detailed in Scenario 2. Identity owners have to be enabled to express whom exactly they want to make specific user profile data available to. That is, it has to be possible to treat any agent authenticated via WebID differently when accessing data of the identity owner's profile. This asks for a flexible mechanism to create customized views on WebID profiles. It has to allow defining both specific profile parts and specific profile requesters. Due to the issues mentioned in Scenario 3 with respect to migrating WebID profiles to new hosts, such mechanism for creating customized profile views also has to produce portable as well as maintainable view definitions.

To protect WebID profiles from unwanted access, data retrievals or tracking attempts [5], the identity owner could set access control rights for WebID profile resources [18]. Yet, existing mechanisms only provide coarse access control. They focus on resources instead of represented data. So, enabling fine-grained access control requires outsourcing WebID profile data to separate resources and set proper permissions. This kind of profile data distribution, however, increases complexity, and complicates modifications and transfers to other systems [22].

Based on the analysis of scenarios Scenarios 1 to 3 and existing mechanisms, we infer that a fine-grained protection against retrieving user profile data by specific subjects has to be flexible, portable, and maintainable. Defining filters on profile data for specific requesters must be flexible and expressive. Identity owners must be enabled to easily transfer filter specifications to other systems without making major adjustments. Filter processors have to be either available or easy to implement within new ecosystems. Filters on profile data must be standard-compliant to ease maintenance and avoid introducing too much overhead.

As outlined in Scenario 4, identity owners want to secure their user profile data against tampering. While identity owners cannot completely prevent or rule out WebID profile data manipulation by malicious server operators or hackers, they want to be aware of unintended changes to their profiles. We consider moving from a managed WebID profile hoster to an own server not as an option here. Profiles hosted on servers the identity owners own can also be vulnerable to attacks, due to security holes at a different system level. To allow subjects to detect profile data tampering, a mechanism to prove the profile's data validity has to be integrated into the authentication process. In consequence of Scenario 5, a WebID profile has to be useless without a proof of its integrity by the identity owner. The fact that malicious manipulations of WebID profile data can happen on a temporary as well as on a permanent basis (cf. Scenario 6) necessitates checking such a proof of correctness on every attempt to access the WebID profile.

To protect WebID profiles from malicious changes of sensitive user data, the identity owner could digitally sign the WebID profile. However, signing a WebID profile at the resource level is bound to a particular representation of this WebID profile, such as *N-Triples*[3], *Notation3*[4] or *RDF/XML*[5]. In addition to the representation of the profile data, also the order of elements (RDF triples) is an important factor. A different element order would change the hash[6] calculated from the resource. That is, it is required to sign the RDF graph or subgraph of the WebID profile [7]. To avoid identity theft, as described in Scenario 5, the WebID certificate could be signed by a trusted certificate authority, which can verify the corresponding WebID profile. This causes a complex process of creating a new tamper-proof protected WebID. A WebID identity owner like Alice can sign her WebID profile using her private key that corresponds to the public key within the WebID certificate and profile. Storing this digital signature within her WebID profile does not protect the WebID profile. This is because an attacker can exchange the public key stored in the WebID profile with his own. Then, he can sign the WebID profile with his own private key.

From the discussion above, we derive the need to create tamper-proof WebID profiles that are universally and easily applicable, backward-compatible and independent of the specific WebID profile representation. Such tampering protection must ensure that data within a WebID profile was created by the WebID identity owner and not by an attacker. It also has to secure WebID profile against identity theft. The process of WebID authentication and retrieving a WebID profile should be modified as little as possible in order to simplify the integration of the protection. This also facilitates backward compatibility with WebID identity providers that do not provide this feature. Creation of a tamper-proof WebID profile should not come at the cost of additional effort for the users.

Delegating a task to a subject to do something on the delegator's behalf is a process involving some risks. The identity owner wants another subject to act in her name, i.e., the delegator officially authorizes the delegatee. That is, the identity owner has to trust another subject at least partially that the authorization is properly used within the intended scope. However, this cannot be guaranteed and, thus, we have to take the worst case into account As described in Scenario 7 a delegatee should be enabled to access to the identity owner's user profile data in the context of WebID. The delegator's WebID profile contains data that might be required by other services and subjects when acting in her name. While it is possible to create a copy of the delegator's WebID profile for particular delegatees, this causes issues like information redundancy and inconsistency due to lost updates of profile data. Having only one WebID profile - and, therefore, one WebID URI - that is used by the identity owner as well as the delegatees requires a fine-grained access control to identify the *real* subject. Apart from this, Scenario 8 exemplifies that the identity owner has to be in the position to control

---

[3] N-Triples: A line-based syntax for RDF graphs, http://www.w3.org/TR/n-triples/.

[4] Notation3 (N3): A readable RDF syntax, http://www.w3.org/TeamSubmission/n3/.

[5] RDF/XML syntax specification, http://www.w3.org/TR/REC-rdf-syntax/.

[6] Besides the identity owner's private key, a hash is the basis of the digital signature.

the lifetime of a particular delegation. This would enable to limit improper use outside the delegator's intended time frame being required to complete the task. In addition to controlling the validity period of a delegation, we can derive from Scenario 9 the requirement of restricting a delegation to specific services. While detecting and enforcing a time restriction is rather simple in this context, identifying a specific service might be a more complex undertaking.

Concluding the analysis of Scenarios 7 to 9 indicates that there is a need for additional protection of identity owners against improper use of their WebID profile data in the context of delegation. A mechanism realizing this protection has to detect who is requesting access to a service, i.e., either the *real* identity owner or one of the delegatees acting on the identity owner's behalf. Even though a delegatee is acting on an identity owner's behalf and only using the identity owner's data, it is important to be aware of the actor and not just the identity owner. The awareness resulting from this detection allows for logging activities of delegatees and, consequently, improving transparency and traceability for the identity owner. To support enforcing the identity owner's intended scope of delegation, appropriate measures have to be available.

Bottom line. The analysis shows that there are three main manifestations of the problem. They include the disclosure of user data to unknown and unwanted subjects retrieving the WebID profile. As another manifestation of the problem, there is a risk of user data manipulation and even identity theft by malicious server operators or subjects that hacked the WebID profile host. Finally, we identified a third manifestation in terms of improper use of user profile data. Especially in delegation scenarios, user profile data is vulnerable to improper use by subjects that act on the identity owner's behalf.

We can trace all problem manifestations back to insufficiently protected WebID profile data. WebID identity owners have to be supported in protecting their user profile data from this problem. It is necessary to create appropriate mechanisms that assist identity owners in securing their sensitive data in a flexible, maintainable, and easy to use way.

4 Protecting WebID Profile Data with ProProtect3

On the basis of the analysis results, we propose the ProProtect3 approach. ProProtect3 is a threefold approach dealing with the problem of insufficiently protected WebID profile data. As this problem has three different manifestations in terms of unwanted retrieval, malicious manipulation, and improper use of WebID profile data, ProProtect3 treats each of them with particular attention.

For integrating the approach into the WebID authentication sequence, we extend the original process illustrated in Fig. 2. There, Alice wanted to retrieve an access-controlled resource and had to authenticate with her WebID certificate before. Our extension to this process by the ProProtect3 approach is highlighted in Fig. 3 and Fig. 4. Here, ① to ⑤ are analogous to Fig. 2. The ProProtect3 approach adds ⑥ and ⑦, as shown in Fig. 3. These two extra steps are responsible for coping with the problem of insufficient protection through verifying both the profile data integrity and the delegation rights stored within the

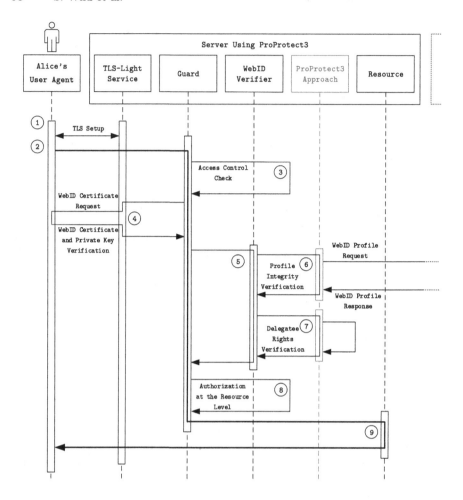

Fig. 3. ProProtect3 Approach for Service Providers

identity owner's WebID profile. Both allow detecting tampering and improper use of user profile data of WebID identity owners. As an example, this assists discovering malicious requests originating by profile data compromised by attackers, e.g., Mallory as server operator, or subjects acting in the identity owner's name. In addition to these verifications, ProProtect3 adds a mechanism to avoid unwanted disclosure of user profile data, as depicted in Fig. 4. All three parts of the approach are complementary and help to increase the protection of user profile data. Unlike both verification mechanisms that are integrated on the service provider's system, the protection against unwanted disclosure is only available on the server hosting the identity owner's WebID profile. Since the server hosting the WebID profile serves incoming profile requests as well, the verification mechanisms could be also integrated there in order to check requests initiated by subjects authenticated via WebID.

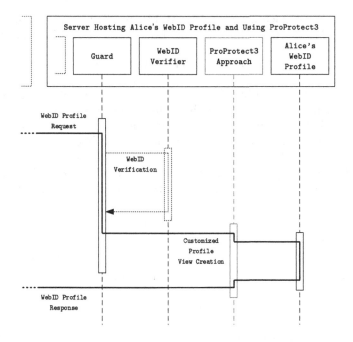

Fig. 4. ProProtect3 Approach for WebID Profile Hosters

The next three sections detail these parts of the ProProtect3 approach. While Sect. 5 provides a solution against unwanted retrieval attempts (cf. Fig. 4), Sect. 6 explains how WebID profiles can be secured from malicious manipulation by offering an integrity protection (cf. ⑥ in Fig. 3). Section 7 presents the third part of the ProProtect3 approach. There, we show our idea for avoiding improper use by subjects acting on behalf of the identity owner (cf. ⑦ in Fig. 3).

5   Protecting User Profile Data from Unwanted Retrieval

To improve the protection of WebID profiles, this part of the ProProtect3 approach defines and applies a fine-grained filtering of data marked as sensitive by the identity owner. We first present the conceptual model for preventing unwanted retrieval of user profile data which we then extend by a technical description.

5.1   Conceptual Contribution to Avoid Unwanted Retrieval

To avoid unwanted retrieval of profile data, we apply a filtering as a graph-to-graph transformation. A WebID profile, e.g., Alice's profile in Fig. 3, acts as filter input. It is represented by graph $G(V, E)$, as formalized in (2). Filter s maps graph G to graph G' depending on identity $i \in I$, as defined by Eq. (6).

$$s : \mathfrak{G} \times I \to \mathfrak{G} \qquad (6)$$

Graph G' represents identity owner's m WebID profile filtered by sensitive data requester $r \in I$ is *not* allowed to retrieve. Equation (7) formalizes this filter.

$$s(G, r) = G' = (V' \subseteq V, E' \subseteq E) \tag{7}$$

This part of the approach handles sensitive data as a subset of triples $T \sim G$. While all sensitive data is available in graph G, requester r is only allowed to see data that is present in graph G'. Filter function f defines a mapping of a set of triples on $\{0, 1\}$ depending on the identity. While "1" means sensitive data and, therefore, that the set of triples is present in graph G', "0" means the opposite. Consequently, whitelisting or blacklisting of sensitive WebID profile data for particular requesters can be achieved using filter function f as defined by (8).

$$f : I \times \{t\} \rightarrow \{0, 1\}, t \in T \tag{8}$$

Function f yields 1 for each triple in graph G and identity owner m. Filter $s(G, r)$ uses f to create filtered graph G' based on G for requester r. RDF triples $T' \subseteq T$ span graph $G' = (V', E'), T' \sim G'$ as defined in Eq. (9).

$$T' = \{t | f_r(t) = 1, t \in T\} \tag{9}$$

To relieve identity owner m from the need to define filter function f_r for each potential r, we introduce fallback function $F(r)$ that yields the best possible fallback entity for a given requester r. Possible fallback entities are:

- *requesters* authenticated using WebID $Z \subseteq I$,
- *specific requesters* defined by the identity owner $S \subseteq Z$,
- requesters who are *friends* of the identity owner $K \subseteq Z$, and
- *anonymous requesters* $A \subseteq I, A \cap Z = \emptyset$.

Let $R = \{k, z, a, n\}$ be a set of special entities: k for friend, z for authenticated user, a for anonym, n for null. Equation (10) formalizes fallback function $F(r)$.

$$F(r) = e = \begin{cases} r & \text{if } \exists f_r \\ k & \text{if } \exists f_k \land r \in K \land r \notin S \\ z & \text{if } \exists f_z \land r \in Z \land r \notin S \land r \notin K \qquad e \in (R \cup S) \\ a & \text{if } \exists f_a \land r \in A \\ n & \text{if } \nexists f_r \land \nexists f_k \land \nexists f_u \land \nexists f_a \end{cases} \tag{10}$$

Filter function f_n, cf. Eq. (11), implements a behavior as if no filtering is active. This enables accessing profiles having no predefined filters.

$$f_n(t) = 1 \; \forall t \in T \tag{11}$$

To use $F(r)$ as part of $s(G, r)$, we refine Eq. (9) as shown in Eq. (12).

$$s(G, F(r)) = G' \sim T' = \{t | f_{F(r)}(t) = 1, t \in T\} \tag{12}$$

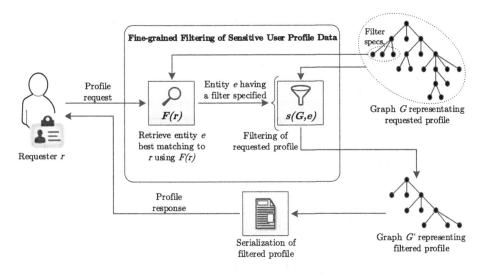

Fig. 5. ProProtect3 for Protecting WebID Profile Data Against Unwanted Disclosure

Figure 5 illustrates the theoretical foundation for this part of our solution, which has been extended from a first design proposed in [42]. It provides a detailed view on the mechanism used in Fig. 4. When requester r tries to retrieve data from the WebID profile of identity owner m, an appropriate filter is searched for requester r using $F(r)$. To protect sensitive profile data, identity owner m has to specify eligible filters prior to this step. Filters are stored as filter specifications in the identity owner's WebID profile. Filter specifications are hidden from anyone but identity owner m. Otherwise, this information is a potential subject to social engineering, e.g., profile analyzers could conclude group affiliations utilizing knowledge about f_r or $F(r)$. Each filter specification consists of entity e and filter s. Having detected a specification for e using $F(r)$, the filter $s(G, e)$ converts graph G into graph G' that represents a WebID profile filtered by data marked as sensitive by m. That is, the profile retrieved by requester r contains only data which satisfies the constraints defined by filter function $f_{F(r)}$.

5.2 Technical Contribution to Avoid Unwanted Retrieval

For implementing this part of the ProProtect3 approach, we introduce the *WebID Profile Filter Language* (WPFL) and use the SPARQL CONSTRUCT query form [21] as transformation and filter function. While we could have implemented the filter facility using proprietary technologies like C#, we favored SPARQL for the sake of homogeneity to the underlying profile data representation as RDF triples. WPFL defines a filter specification. It consists of three elements: *entity name* for e, *filter command* for $s(G, e)$ and a *specification element* to bind them together and connect the filter to the WebID profile. The specification element allows storing filter specifications either in the owner's profile, i.e., graph G, or separately as linked resources. These elements are described by three RDF triples, as exemplarily shown in Turtle[7] syntax below:

```
1  <WEBID URI> filter:specification [
2    filter:entity ENTITY;
3    filter:command COMMAND
4  ] .
```

The SPARQL CONSTRUCT query form facilitates constructing a new graph G' based on an existing graph G, as required by Eq. (7). It can include or exclude data during construction of $G' \sim T'$ and, hence, implements Eq. (9). A whitelisting - as defined by this equation - mentioning all data to be available in graph G' is described by following filter command[8]:

```
1  CONSTRUCT { ?s ?p ?o } FROM <WEBID URI> WHERE { ?s ?p ?o .
2    FILTER(?s in (Subject1, Subject2, [...])) .
3    FILTER(?p in (Predicate1, Predicate2, [...])) .
4    FILTER(?o in (Object1, Object2, [...]))
5  }
```

As an example, if solely the foaf:knows predicate is mentioned, all contacts are copied from G to G'. To increase filtering granularity, it is beneficial to also mention subjects or objects of RDF triples, e.g., in order to include/exclude specific contacts. This all together defines one *filter directive*. SPARQL's UNION keywords enable to use several filter directives in one filter command. We utilize SPARQL Property Path [33] to cover filtering of context-dependent data. For instance, street data could be context-dependent as they are element of an address, which in turn could be element of either private or business contact data. Property paths help to address relevant elements in graph G by specifying the routes between them. For example, a filter command to construct a new graph by including name and image of identity owner m as well as city and country of his/her home - but not street, postal code etc. - is described as follows[9]:

```
1  CONSTRUCT { ?s ?p ?o } FROM <WEBID URI> WHERE {
2    {?s ?p ?o . FILTER(?p in (foaf:name, foaf:img))} UNION
3    {?s ?p ?o . ?t con:home ?o} UNION
4    {?s ?p ?o . ?t con:home/con:address ?o} UNION
5    {?s ?p ?o . ?t con:home/con:address/con:city ?o} UNION
6    {?s ?p ?o . ?t con:home/con:address/con:country ?o}
7  }
```

---

[7] Turtle Terse RDF Triple Language, http://www.w3.org/TeamSubmission/turtle/.

[8] In contrast to whitelisting, blacklisting data is also supported by SPARQL CONSTRUCT queries via MINUS statements.

[9] Lines 3 and 4 create the context needed to include city and country. Address data is described via the PIM ontology, http://www.w3.org/2000/10/swap/pim/contact#.

A dedicated SPARQL query uses the identity information provided by requester r to select the best-matching available filter specification based on the retrieved filter entity, as formalized in Eq. (10). Once an appropriate filter specification is selected, the corresponding filter command is directly passed to a SPARQL processor that executes the graph-to-graph transformation.

6   Protecting User Profile Data from Malicious Change

To improve the protection of WebID profiles against malicious manipulation, this part of the ProProtect3 approach provides three components to enable the data integrity verification of WebID profiles. Being aware that the data integrity of potentially third-party hosted profiles cannot be protected, we aim at making malicious manipulations visible to requesters and the identity owner. First, we need to digitally sign the WebID profile for guaranteeing its authenticity and integrity. Signing a WebID profile ensures that the statements provided in the profile originate from the WebID identity owner [30]. Second, to prevent malicious change of the public key, it must be bound to the WebID profile in an unchangeable manner. Finally, the WebID authentication sequence needs to be extended on this foundation to support automatic data integrity checks of requested WebID profiles. We present the conceptual model for the first two components which we then use for a technical description of the third component.

6.1   Conceptual Contribution to Detect Malicious Manipulation

As WebID profile data can be expressed through RDF triples in various ways using different syntaxes, we focus on RDF graphs that are the basis of WebID profiles and use the equivalence formalized in Eq. (2). The ProProtect3 approach defines a signature for each filtered representation of the WebID profile (cf. Sect. 5). Carroll proposed in [7] how to sign a graph in a complexity of $\mathcal{O}(n \log n)$. Each filtered representation of a WebID profile builds a new graph which can be signed. The procedure of signing a Minimum Self-contained Graph (MSG) suggested by Tummarello et al. in [40] does not fit to our approach, because the filters, described in Sect. 5, could exclude some blank nodes of a MSG. Blank nodes in RDF are nodes without a URI reference and aggregate concepts like a person's address [28]. So, an agent verifying the integrity of a WebID profile could receive a filtered representation of that profile, where some blank nodes of a MSG are missing. Verifying the signature of the filtered profile would fail because it was generated with blank nodes inside the graph [40]. Yet, the profile data still originates from the correct subject, i.e., the identity owner.

In the ProProtect3 approach, signing a WebID profile involves four steps: The first step consists in triggering the actual signing for each filter specified in a given WebID profile. When the identity owner, like Alice, creates a new filter for her profile data, this filter will be executed to generate the customized view on her profile. Afterwards, the filtered profile data will be signed and the signature will be attached to the filter. When WebID profile data is changed by the identity owner, each existing filter needs to be executed and each customized profile view $G' \in \mathfrak{G}'$, where $\mathfrak{G}'$ is the set of all filtered graphs of one profile, has to be signed once again, as formalized in Eq. (13).

$$\mathfrak{G}' = \{G'|G' = s(G, e), e \in (R \cup S)\} \tag{13}$$

Without changing the semantic of the filtered WebID profile G', the second step transforms it into a canonical representation G'_c, as formalized in Eq. (14).

$$c(G') = G'_c \sim T'_c \ \forall G' \in \mathfrak{G}' \tag{14}$$

In the third step, we sign the filtered WebID profile in canonical representation G'_c and attach the signature to the corresponding filter. To sign G'_c, we combine the hashes of each statement $h(t_x)$ into a single value. The hash of a statement is computed by concatenating the hashes of each subject, predicate and object, which then will be hashed again, as formalized in Eq. (15). While Kasten and Scherp in [26] create an overall hash of the sorted hashes, we deterministically canonize the filtered WebID profile in ProProtect3. So, the hashes of all statements can be concatenated again and a new hash can be calculated from them.

$$h(T'_c) = h\left(\sum h(t)\right) \forall t \in T'_c \tag{15}$$

This hash of an entire filtered WebID profile and the main private key k'^{-1} of the identity owner are used to create the signature of a filtered WebID profile, as formalized in Eq. (16). A WebID profile can contain several public keys K of the identity owners. The identity owner also owns the corresponding WebID certificates and private keys. However, she can choose a main asymmetric key pair (k', k'^{-1}) which is specially used to sign and verify the WebID profile data.

$$sig = a(k'^{-1}, h(T'_c)) \tag{16}$$

In the fourth and final step, the signature sig is attached to the filter so that the original WebID profile remains unchanged and the existing signatures of other filters are still valid. If an agent requests a filtered WebID profile, our approach responds with the requested filtered profile and the corresponding signature.

This part of ProProtect3 addresses protection against identity theft by putting the identity owner's main public key k' inside the WebID URI. As signing a WebID profile is insufficient to protect it against identity theft (cf. Scenario 5), also verifying the signature of the WebID profile would fail. An attacker could sign the WebID profile once again with his own private key that is associated to the public key he recently added to the attacked WebID profile. By binding the identity owner's main public key $k' \in K$ to her WebID URI w', as formalized by Eq. (17) using function g, changing the main public key would invalidate the owner's WebID identity $i = (w', T)$.

$$g(w') = k' \tag{17}$$

6.2   Technical Contribution to Detect Malicious Manipulation

ProProtect3 utilizes the WebID URI for storing the main public key, as defined by Eq. (17), in a SHA-256 hashed form. Using a hash for the main public key k' is both easily applicable and secure against identity theft. Depending on the key strength, public keys can be quite long, e.g., 2048-bit or 4096-bit. Here, a hashed version is much shorter, e.g., 256-bit, without sacrificing security. This makes integrity-enabled WebID URIs more manageable. We convert the hashed public key via Base64 encoding with URL and filename safe alphabet [25] The ProProtect3 approach uses the SHA-256 hash function which extends the WebID URI by 44 characters.

To transform the filtered WebID profile G' into a canonical representation, as defined in Eq. (14), the RDF graph of the filtered WebID profile is transformed into the N-Triples notation. This notation has to be sorted in lexicographic order, because transforming an RDF graph into N-Triples notation does not indicate any sort. A deterministic sort is needed to compute the same hash value of the same graph. Afterwards, the one-step deterministic labeling proposed by Carroll in [7] is applied to name blank nodes in a deterministic fashion. This is necessary because the same blank node could have different identifiers without changing the semantics. That is, different identifiers would cause different hash values calculated from the same filtered WebID profile.

Detecting malicious manipulation of WebID profile data requires extending the WebID authentication sequence by the new security features described above. Since this part of ProProtect3 deals with verifying the integrity of WebID profiles, the corresponding process is illustrated by ⑥ in Fig. 3. To get a more detailed view, Fig. 6 focuses on the verification process and, thus, only shows the WebID verifier and Alice's WebID profile to provide context and facilitate understanding.

Verification starts when the WebID verifier is called to verify a subject's proof of identity. As usual, Alice uses her WebID certificate as a potential proof of identity. The WebID verifier transmits Alice's WebID certificate to ProProtect3 for validating the integrity of her WebID profile (cf. ① in Fig. 6). ProProtect3 then extracts the WebID URI referring to Alice's WebID profile from the subject alternative name field inside her WebID certificate [9, 34].

ProProtect3 requests Alice's WebID profile from the hosting server specified by the WebID URI afterwards (cf. ②). In case the hosting server has a matching filter for the request, the filter will be applied to Alice's WebID profile before responding with that profile. Otherwise, Alice's WebID profile is included to the response without filtering the profile (cf. ③). The corresponding signature of the filtered or not filtered WebID profile is attached to the response. ProProtect3 extracts the hashed public key from inside the WebID URI. If Alice's WebID profile is not integrity protected using the ProProtect3 approach, then there is no hash available inside the WebID URI and ProProtect3 falls back to the standard verification of a WebID profile defined by the WebID specification [34].

For each public key listed in Alice's WebID profile, the same hash function is computed and compared with the hash value from the URI (cf. ④). If a hash

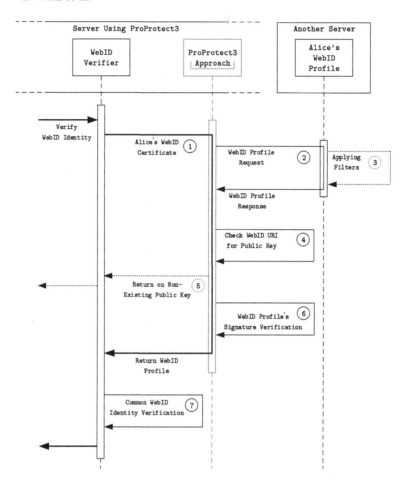

Fig. 6. ProProtect3 for Protecting WebID Profile Data Against Tampering

value of one public key equals to the hash value in the URI, this is the main public key, which can be used to verify the signature of Alice's WebID profile. In case there is no matching hash value, this indicates that Alice's profile data has been manipulated without her knowledge. This would result in a failed verification of Alice's WebID identity. A failure notification would be sent by ProProtect3 to the WebID verifier, which declares the WebID verification as failed (cf. ⑤).

On the contrary, ProProtect3 successfully verifies the signature of Alice's WebID profile with her main public key. The hash of this WebID profile is generated in the way described above. The integrity of Alice's WebID profile can be verified (cf. ⑥) using the signature, the generated hash of the received WebID profile, and the main public key. If the signature verification fails, then ProProtect3 sends a failure notification to the WebID verifier. Otherwise, ProProtect3 passes Alice's WebID profile to the WebID verifier. The WebID verifier then checks Alice's profile as defined in WebID specification (cf. ⑦ in Fig. 6).

7   Protecting User Profile Data from Improper Use

To fulfill the protection needs we identified in the analysis from the early beginning, we designed a new delegation procedure that considers them as integral parts. We first present the conceptual model for preventing improper use of profile data in delegation scenarios which we then extend by a technical description.

7.1   Conceptual Contribution to Prevent Improper Use

For defining the delegation roles, the ProProtect3 approach reuses the WebID artifacts as shown in Fig. 7. Here, a delegator i_A, like Alice, enables a delegatee i_C, like Casey, to act on her behalf. This is formalized in Eq. (18), where w_A is

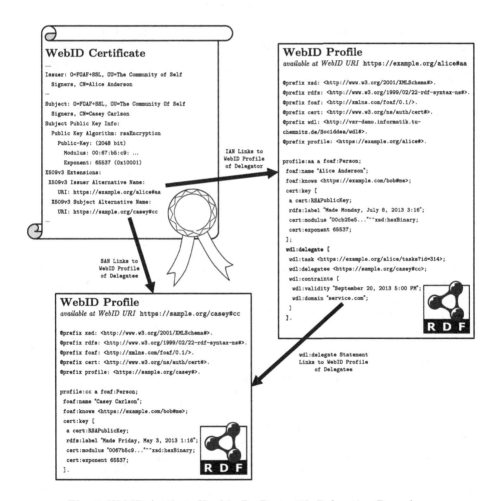

Fig. 7. WebID Artifacts Used in ProProtect3's Delegation Procedure

the delegator's WebID URI, T_A represents the delegator's WebID profile, w_C is the delegatee's WebID URI, and T_C represents the delegatee's profile.

$$i_A = (w_A, T_A) \quad i_C = (w_C, T_C) \quad i_A, i_C \in I; w_A, w_C \in W; T_A, T_C \in \mathfrak{T} \quad (18)$$

While a delegator's WebID certificate is according to Eq. (4), a delegatee's WebID certificate $C_{i_C, k_C} \in C_{i_C}$ is as formalized in Eq. (19), where $C_{i_C} \in \mathfrak{C}$ is the set of WebID certificates owned by identity i_C and $\mathfrak{C}$ the set of all WebID certificates. Not only does the delegatee's WebID certificate contain the delegatee's WebID URI w_C and a public key k_C owned by the delegatee, but also the WebID URI w_A denoting the delegator i_A. As usual, WebID certificate C_{i_C, k_C} is signed with the corresponding private key k_C^{-1} or the private key of a trusted party.

$$C_{i_C, k_C, w_A} = (w_C, k_C, w_A) \quad (19)$$

When the delegatee authenticates to a service with such certificate C_{i_C, k_C}, it can use the delegator's WebID w_A stored within the certificate to dereference the delegator's WebID profile represented by T_A. The delegator's profile contains a set of delegations D_A specified by delegator i_A. While D_A is described by triples $T_{A,D} \subset T_A$, each delegation $d_{w_C}^j \in D_A$ is described by triples $T_{A,d} \subseteq T_{A,D}$. Delegation $d_{w_C}^j$, defined in Eq. (20), involves a task j to be done by delegatee i_C, referred to by WebID URI w_C, taking a set of constraints Q into account. This allows delegatee i_C for acting on behalf of delegator i_A (cf. Eq. (21)).

$$d_{w_C}^j = (j, w_C, Q) \quad (20)$$

$$i_C \text{ can act on behalf of } i_A \Leftrightarrow \exists w_A, w_C : \exists d_{w_C}^j \in D_A, \exists C_{i_C, k_C, w_A} \quad (21)$$

7.2   Technical Contribution to Prevent Improper Use

To identify the *real* subject which is using a service (cf. Scenario 7), ProProtect3 adds identifiers for both delegator Alice and delegatee Casey to a WebID certificate (cf. Eq. (19)). Here, ProProtect3 does not change the original semantics of a WebID certificate because the *Subject Alternative Name* (SAN) field of the certificate still contains the WebID URI denoting the subject that will primarily use a service. In the delegation context, this is delegatee Casey i_C. In addition to the rather common data contained in Casey's WebID certificate, the ProProtect3 delegation procedure exploits the *Issuer* and the *Issuer Alternative Name* (IAN) certificate fields. They are used to denote the delegator Alice i_A, i.e., by her name and her WebID URI w_A referring to her WebID profile (cf. Eq. (18)).

While Casey's WebID profile, represented by T_C, remains as it is, Alice's WebID profile, represented by T_A, needs to be extended for storing further delegation parameters (cf. Eq. (20)). This extension is necessary to prevent attackers to act in Alice's name by creating such *"delegation-enabled WebID certificate"*, cf. Eq. (19), on their own. Since Alice is the initiator of a delegation, we think this extension of her WebID profile is justified. Although it is possible to store such delegation statements in other resources Alice owns or trusts, the ProProtect3 delegation procedure needs to be aware of them when processing a request of a service trying to retrieve them. To be consistent with the vision of a distributed online social network, the delegation parameters should at least be linked to. For these reasons, it is recommended to include either the entire set of delegation parameters or a reference to it in Alice's WebID profile.

Addressing the analysis results of Scenarios 7, 8, 9, we introduce the *WebID Delegation Language (WDL)* to specify a delegation's task, its associated restrictions, and the potential delegatee that should work on the task on the delegator's behalf (cf. Eq. (20)). WDL is a vocabulary that can be expressed through RDF. In WDL the description of a `task` is a URI pointing to a resource containing further information about the work to be done. It is not included directly in WDL to allow flexible descriptions and meta data to be attached to a task. The way tasks are actually described is outside the scope of this article. WDL enables delegators, like Alice, to define `constraints` regarding `validity` and `domain` of a delegation. Here, the validity is represented by a time stamp indicating the end of a delegation and, thus, the deadline of the assigned task. The WDL domain constraint defines a restriction of services that Alice authorizes Casey to use in her name. That is, by specifying the domain name of a service, Casey is only allowed to do the task within this particular domain. WDL assists identifying a `delegatee` through a WebID URI by means of another RDF triple. The structure of WDL is exemplarily shown in Turtle syntax below:

```
1  <WEBID URI OF DELEGATOR> wdl:delegate [
2    wdl:task <URI POINTING TO TASK DESCRIPTION>;
3    wdl:contraints [
4      wdl:validity DEADLINE;
5      wdl:domain SERVICE
6    ];
7    wdl:delegatee <WEBID URI OF DELEGATEE> ].
```

By providing the definition of the WebID artifacts and vocabulary that are used in the ProProtect3 delegation procedure, the foundation to implement the delegation process has been created. It is described in the following.

Process of delegation. A successful task delegation requires (1) initializing the delegation, (2) notifying potential delegatees, (3) accepting the delegation, (4) performing the task by a delegatee on behalf of the delegator, (5) controlling as well as monitoring, and (6) terminating the delegation.

Initializing a delegation. In the ProProtect3 approach, the process of delegation is driven by the delegator. Even though it is possible to switch the roles driving the delegation, a delegator-driven procedure has various advantages regarding the process' purposefulness and the protection of a delegator's user profile data. These advantages will become evident in the following.

Alice as a delegator has to formalize her intention that another subject, like Casey, should act on her behalf. Therefore, she defines the parameters of a delegation using WDL. While we recommend assisting this formalization by a graphical user dialog, this is not a part of our approach and depends on the WebID identity providers and managers implementing it.

Notifying potential delegatees. Knowing Casey's WebID URI that Alice assigned to the `delegatee` property in the WDL delegation parameters allows exploiting further information about Casey on the basis of his WebID profile. That is, Alice can inform Casey about her request to act on her behalf using one of Casey's preferred communication methods that are outlined in his profile. Similar to the initialization of a delegation, also the notification can be supported through appropriate techniques provided by the service integrating ProProtect3.

Accepting a delegation. Given that Casey received Alice's notification, he can read the description of the task Alice intends to entrust him with and, consequently, either accept or reject her request. If Casey decides to work on this task on behalf of Alice, he can create a delegation-enabled WebID certificate in the way described above, containing both Alice's and his own WebID URI. We recommend assisting this step by automatically generating such certificate. WebID identity providers could issue a certificate like this when Casey visits Alice's profile. Since Casey's WebID URI is stored within the delegation parameters in Alice's WebID profile and Casey's WebID URI would be available through authentication using his WebID certificate, a WebID identity provider could easily detect this connection and take appropriate measures.

Executing a delegation. Having issued a delegation-enabled WebID certificate to Casey, he can authenticate to a service that supports WebID authentication and integrates ProProtect3. Figure 8 illustrates the authentication sequence as a more detailed view of Figs. 3 and 4, but only focuses on the components and activities that are important for this part of the approach. When Casey tries authenticating to a server using ProProtect3, his valid delegation-enabled WebID certificate is passed from the WebID verifier to ProProtect3 in ①. ProProtect3 parses Casey's WebID certificate and extracts both his WebID URI and Alice's one from the certificate's SAN and IAN field. Casey's WebID profile is requested in ②. As neither Casey's WebID URI nor his WebID profile include a sign of integrity protection, ProProtect3 cannot attest in ③ that his profile data was not manipulated. Alice's WebID profile is requested in ④. Since Alice hosts her WebID profile on a server that integrates ProProtect3, a customized view on her profile data is automatically created in ⑤. This view on her profile data is specific to the WebID identity which is used by the service requesting her profile. The service is not aware of this profile customization. In ⑥, the integrity of Alice's profile is verified by our approach. Since Alice's WebID URI suggests that her WebID profile data is integrity-protected, ProProtect3 will abort the authentication when it finds any sign for manipulation (cf. Sect. 6). If the verification is successful, both WebID profiles are passed to the WebID verifier.

The delegation parameters are analyzed in ⑦ using Alice's WebID profile, which has been retrieved before. They must contain Casey's WebID URI. Otherwise, the verification of the delegation rights fails, i.e., either the entire authentication fails or Casey is allowed to use the service on his own but *not* on Alice's behalf. This decision depends on the implementation of ProProtect3 by the service. The delegation constraints defined by Alice are checked in ⑧ and ⑨. Once a constraint verification fails, the delegation fails as well and, similar to the failed delegation rights check discussed above, possibly the entire authentication.

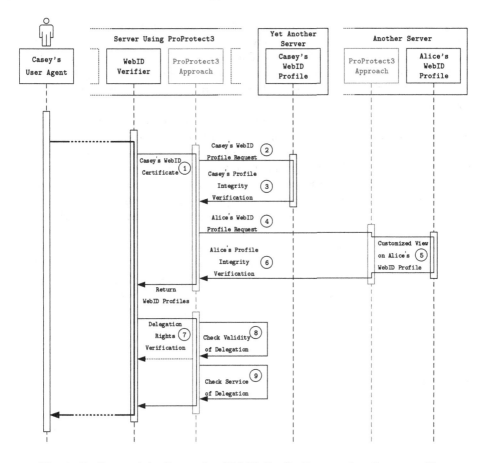

Fig. 8. ProProtect3 for Protecting WebID Profile Data against Improper Use

Provided a successful authentication and delegation, Casey can perform the task using this service on Alice's behalf, as defined in Eq. (21). Even though the service can access Alice's profile data, Casey might have a customized view on her WebID profile caused by filtering of profile data, as shown in ⑤ and described in Sect. 5.

Monitoring a delegation. Similar to other digital or traditional delegation procedures, it is possible that Casey will face problems while working on a task entrusted to him by Alice. Casey could discuss these issues with Alice to find an appropriate solution or she could support him by adjusting the deadline associated to the delegation accordingly.

Under certain circumstances, however, it is important to know the progress made by the delegatee independently from his personal status reports (cf. Scenario 7). For this purpose, Alice wants to login to the service used by Casey for accomplishing this task. In the ProProtect3 delegation procedure the delegator and the delegatee acting on the delegator's behalf are handled as individual subjects having two different WebID identities each consisting of an individual URI, profile, and certificate. This enables Alice to authenticate to the service as well via her own WebID identity. When the service is offering status indicators or activity logs to customers, then Alice can find out about Casey's progress with respect to the task assigned to him. Offering such mechanisms, however, is the service's responsibility.

Terminating a delegation. As soon as Casey has completed the task on the delegator's behalf before the deadline, he can optionally inform Alice about this success using a suitable communication channel. If Casey was not able to finish the task within the given time frame, then the delegation to act in Alice's name is no longer valid. As a consequence, ProProtect3 will not allow Casey to work on the task after passing the deadline. The proposed approach also enables Alice to terminate the delegation at any time. This might be necessary when the task is expendable for some reason like priority shifts, when she observes that the delegatee is not performing well and she wants to reassign the task to Dave, or when she wants to do the task on her own. She can do this for the current task by changing or removing the delegatee's WebID URI from the delegation parameters. For all types of completing a delegation it is required that the service using ProProtect3 either checks the authentication or automatically authenticates the delegatee again on a regular basis. This is needed to be aware of updates affecting the delegation.

8   Evaluation

In this section we discuss the evaluation of our approach. Based on the analysis conducted in Sect. 3, we argue that ProProtect3 assists identity owners to improve the protection of their WebID profile data. We pay particular attention to each part of the approach by outlining our expectations and explaining the actual findings, which provide some quite interesting insights.

While the ProProtect3 approach is generic and can be implemented in many systems, we demonstrate it using Sociddea [43]. Sociddea is a WebID identity provider and management platform developed with ASP.NET MVC4. With Sociddea, a user can automatically create a new WebID URI, an underlying WebID profile and an associated client certificate. Although Sociddea allows users to host their WebID profiles in the ecosystem provided by Sociddea, there is no constraint to do this. That is, users are also empowered to create new client certificates for profiles hosted somewhere else. Sociddea can represent a WebID profile in various ways. Figure 9 exemplifies an HTML and RDF/XML representation for the same WebID profile hosted on Sociddea.

Protecting User Profile Data from Unwanted Retrieval. The proposed approach enables profile owners to create filters on their WebID profile for specific requesters or groups of requesters. Sociddea therefore provides a graphical user interface to configure filters for profile data to prevent unwanted disclosure. Identity owners can switch from the common profile authoring to the filter specification mode. Here, all identity attributes presented in the profile authoring

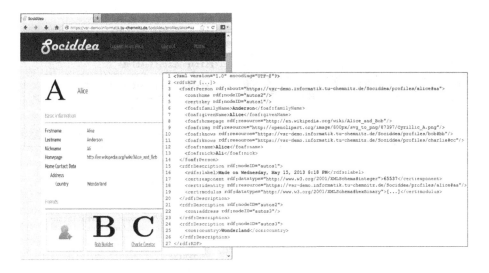

Fig. 9. Representations of a WebID profile hosted on Sociddea

mode can be used for specifying filters, i.e., each available identity attribute can be marked as either visible or hidden. Profile owners can independently include or exclude each RDF triple present in their profile using Sociddea's graphical filter editor, which supports predicate-based filtering, e.g., by first name, last name or phone number. By selecting an available entity, an already existing filter specification is used to visualize the former identity attribute selection by the user. ProProtect3's fine-grained and context-aware filtering facility allows identity owners to create customized profile views for diverse requesting entities. Once the identity owner completed the selection for a specific entity, this configuration is verified and sent to the Sociddea back-end. This fulfills the requirements we have derived from Scenarios 1 and 2.

To enable machines to process this yet informal filter configuration, a SPARQL CONSTRUCT statement is automatically created. Both whitelisting and blacklisting of RDF triples are supported by our solution. We recommend whitelisting, because the exposed filters do not contain any information on hidden profile parts. Exposing this kind of information can cause speculations. Additionally, whitelisting eases constructing an empty graph representation of a profile, which might be relevant for identity owners having stringent requirements for privacy and, thus, want to forbid anonymous profile requests. Our solution also allows creating filters that remove all filter specifications during construction of the profile view. Consequently, profile requesters remain unaware of the filtering. As whitelisting of attributes has been implemented, this SPARQL statement contains all identity attributes declared as visible for the specific entity. All three RDF triples relevant to specify the filter are stored within the identity owner's WebID profile. The process of creating such profile data filter is shown in Fig. 10.

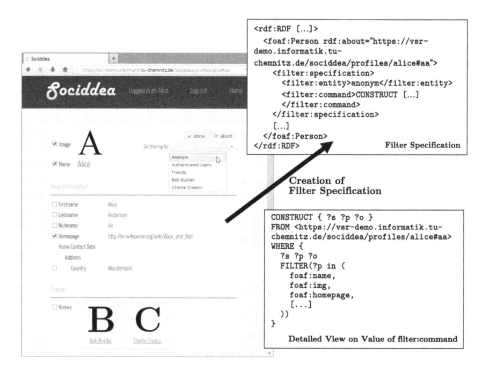

Fig. 10. Creation of Filter Specification Based on User Selection

Although the implementation generates SPARQL CONSTRUCT statements based on the identity attributes selected by the identity owner, the solution is not limited to this. For generating profiles filtered by certain attributes, an identity owner is allowed to use any valid statement. The flexibility of ProProtect3 also allows filtering even identity attributes unsupported by the graphical user interface and facilitates to handle special cases like conditional filtering. Both can be accomplished via appropriate SPARQL commands. Once the filter specification has been created, it is automatically considered during all future attempts to access the particular profile. When a requester tries to retrieve the profile, the solution searches for an appropriate filter specification using the provided identity data and the `filter:entity` triples in the WebID profile. Having found a matching filter entity, the `filter:command` triple belonging to the same `filter:specification` is extracted and directly passed to a SPARQL processor, i.e., no modification is made to the command. While results produced by the SPARQL processor are rendered as defined in the request, rendering as such is not a part of the ProProtect3 approach. Figure 11 exemplifies the filtering of a WebID profile for an anonymous requester using the previously created filter specification.

The proposed solution does not require outsourcing data to separate resources for implementing a flexible filtering. All necessary information can remain in one place. User profile data and filter specifications are independently handled

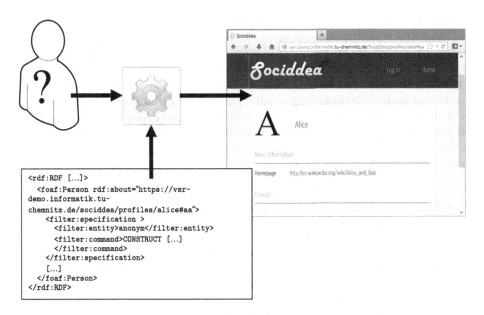

```
<rdf:RDF [...]>
  <foaf:Person rdf:about="https://vsr-
demo.informatik.tu-
chemnitz.de/sociddea/profiles/alice#aa">
    <filter:specification >
      <filter:entity>anonym</filter:entity>
      <filter:command>CONSTRUCT [...]
      </filter:command>
    </filter:specification>
    [...]
  </foaf:Person>
</rdf:RDF>
```

Fig. 11. WebID Profile Data Filtered for Anonymous Requester

in our solution. This simplifies updating, replacing or removing already existing filter specifications. The fallback mechanism $F(r)$ selects the most appropriate filter based on availability and provided identity data. When a specific filter is unavailable, the procedure falls back to an available, more unspecific filter which matches at least some characteristics of the requester. Such fallback mechanism is not part of any related work known to the authors (cf. Sect. 9).

To apply filtering of sensitive profile data by utilizing $s(G, r)$, only the graph representing the WebID profile and the requesting entity are used as input parameters. This part of the ProProtect3 approach introduces only minimal overhead with three RDF triples to define a filter specification for a specific requester. The owner's WebID profile can contain all filter specifications, i.e., while separation between profile data and filter specifications is allowed, it is not required. To further ensure maintainability, we did not develop an own language for filter commands, but use SPARQL as a well-established and proven language. SPARQL allows creating flexible and complex filters, whereas related work tries reducing complexity by defining a restricted vocabulary. We assume that restricted vocabularies offer advantages in terms of usability, but they also limit the possibilities of filtering and cause workarounds, like the necessity of outsourcing sensitive user profile data. Independent of the chosen solution, we expect that common profile owners do not have the skills required to create and maintain filters without assistance through specialized user interfaces.

For seamlessly integrating this part of ProProtect3 into existing systems, filter function f_n implements a behavior as if no filtering were active. This facilitates accessing profiles having no predefined filters. As identity owners are enabled to store all necessary filter details within their WebID profile using our solution, the effort to transfer filter specifications to a new hosting system is reduced (cf. Scenario 3). While other filtering and access control mechanisms, as discussed in Sect. 9, rely on particular interpreters to execute filters, high availability of SPARQL processors for many platforms and architectures contributes to our solution's interoperability and, thus, filter portability. With only minimal additional filtering logic to be interpreted in our ProProtect3 approach, a SPARQL processor can directly apply the WPFL-based filter command to create a new filtered graph. Supported by the fact that these processors were continuously optimized during the last years [29], this allows an efficient execution.

Protecting User Profile Data from Malicious Change. Signing the WebID profile facilitates detecting malicious manipulation of profile data. If Mallory changes the email address or other significant data of Alice in her WebID profile (cf. Scenario 4), verifying the signature of this profile fails because Mallory cannot sign the WebID profile with Alice main private key.

The protection against theft of a WebID identity (cf. Scenario 5) is offered by extending the WebID URI with the SHA-256 hash value of the main public key, which is used for verifying the signature of the WebID profile. There are also hash functions that generate much shorter output, e.g., MD5 (22 characters) or SHA-1 (27 characters). Yet, they are either classified as insecure today or considered to be unsafe in the next years. In contrast, SHA-256 is estimated as secure until 2030 [4]. When Mallory exchanges the main public key in the WebID profile by his own one, he can sign the WebID profile with his corresponding private key, but he cannot change the hash value of the public key in the WebID URI[10]. Changing this hash value changes the identifier of Alice's WebID identity, i.e., her WebID URI. As a failed attack, Mallory would create a new WebID identity instead of hijacking Alice's one. This protection also secures a WebID profile against temporary manipulation or temporary identity theft (cf. Scenario 6).

A limitation of our approach against malicious change is that both the WebID identity provider and the service provider need to integrate ProProtect3. This is necessary for signature creation via the identity provider and for signature verification via the service. An advantage of the ProProtect3 approach is its backward-compatibility. There are two fallback mechanisms to achieve that.

The first fallback mechanism is already applied by following the design of the WebID identification approach. A URI that refers to a ProProtect3-protected WebID profile contains the hash value of the main public key. This URI is still a valid WebID URI. When a ProProtect3-protected WebID identity is verified at a host that does not support our approach, it is still possible to perform the authentication, as specified in [34]. A WebID verifier can request the WebID profile as usual. Furthermore, the signature appended to the WebID profile can be ignored by the WebID verifier without losing any necessary user profile data.

The second mechanism employed in our approach detects when a non-ProProtect3-protected WebID profile needs to be verified. Then, it falls back

---

[10] Since we used security methods considered as safe, it is unlikely to find a collision to the hash value in a WebID URI or to create a private key from a given public key.

to the verification process specified by the W3C. Our approach saves the signature of a filtered WebID profile at the corresponding filter specification. It is therefore not required to recreate all existing signatures when a new filter is added. If data within the WebID profile is changed, only these signatures need to be recreated that are affected by the change of associated customized WebID profile views.

Verifying a ProProtect3-protected WebID profile does not require human interaction. That is, the part of ProProtect3 proposed in Sect. 6 will verify the integrity of a WebID profile by checking the WebID URI and by validating the signature of the WebID profile. Unlike automatic integrity verification, modifying WebID profile data requires the main private key of the identity owner to recreate a valid signature of the updated data. This is a disadvantage of our approach. Losing or compromising the main public/private key pair requires creating a new WebID identity. That is, the identity owner needs to create a new main public/private key pair for signing the profile. Due to the fact that the main public key is encoded inside the WebID URI, the new main public key needs to be stored there, too. Thus, the identity owner would create a new WebID identity by changing the WebID URI.

Protecting User Profile Data from Improper Use. The way we designed the delegation procedure takes protection into account as a first thought. Instead of handing out the delegator's credentials or WebID certificate to a delegatee, the delegatee stays the same person when using a service. A service integrating ProProtect3 can use the delegator's WebID URI, which is additionally stored in the WebID certificate, to retrieve and process the WebID profile data of the delegator, like Alice, on her behalf. Delegator Alice could also define a customized view on her profile data for an identifiable service retrieving her WebID profile. Even though the delegatee authenticates to a service, the delegatee and the service can have a different views on the delegator's user profile data.

This makes interesting use cases possible: A delegatee could have a restricted view on the delegator's profile data, whereas a service used by the delegatee could see further profile data. So, without having access to the delegator's bank account data, a delegatee could perform transactions on the delegator's behalf.

ProProtect3 allows services for clearly distinguishing between individually acting subjects (like Casey as Casey) and subjects acting on behalf of others (like Casey as Alice). When preferred by the identity owner, this distinctness assists fine-grained subject logging and addresses the need identified in Scenario 7.

The delegation facility enabled by ProProtect3 is backward-compatible. We did not change anything on the existing semantics of the artifacts used in WebID. That is, if a system does not integrate the proposed ProProtect3 approach, users can still authenticate with their WebID certificates as usual. However, they will lose benefits like filling forms with the delegator's profile data.

While a WebID identity provider like Sociddea could generate a delegation-enabled WebID certificate pointing to the WebID profiles of both the delegator and the delegatee, they can also be created manually. Compared to a common WebID certificate, the creation effort is almost the same, i.e., it requires only one additional information for exactly referring to the delegator by a WebID URI.

Besides having delegation-enabled WebID certificates, the approach takes the needs into account that are evident in Scenarios 8 and 9. ProProtect3 allows defining delegation constraints within the WebID profile of the delegator. Thus, they are machine-readable. While we considered restricting time and service location of a delegation at the moment, the way the approach handles constraints makes flexible as well as extensible settings possible. That is, it would be easy to add restriction types that become necessary in the future.

Most evaluation results for this part of the approach were positive yet anticipated. Yet, we also discovered some issues: An identity owner must know the person that should act on her behalf by explicitly specifying a WebID URI. Furthermore, an identity owner can only delegate one task per delegatee at the same time. Finally, it is not possible for Bob to *further delegate*[11] a task to Casey, when this task has been delegated to Bob from Alice before. It is controversial whether the last issue is useful or intended. We are convinced that the issues do not disqualify this part of ProProtect3 and can be addressed in future work.

Evaluating this part of the approach for threats and potential attacks indicated that our solution provides a sufficient protection in the context of delegation:

Assuming that Mallory knows about Alice's intent to delegate a task to Casey. He plans to anticipate Casey's confirmation to Alice's request to be in the position to act in her name. Therefore, he creates a new WebID certificate referring to Alice's and his own WebID profile instead of Casey's one. Here, it is worth mentioning that a WebID identity provider integrating ProProtect3 does not support Mallory in creating this certificate. Such identity provider is aware of Alice's *real* delegation target, i.e., Casey, which is specified inside her WebID profile. Thus, it does not offer Mallory the facility to automatically generate a WebID certificate for this delegation when visiting Alice's profile representation. Given that Mallory constructed this WebID certificate on his own, he can authenticate to a service as himself. However, a ProProtect3-enabled service provider does not allow him to act on behalf of Alice because the WebID URI stored within the delegation statement in Alice's WebID profile does not link to Mallory but to Casey. That is, the ProProtect3 approach protects the identity owner against improper use of her user profile data.

At first we thought that the WebID certificate of a delegatee is the perfect place to store the validity constraint specified by the delegator. All X.509 certificates have a validity field to define the *"time interval during which the CA warrants that it will maintain information about the status of the certificate"* [9]. Alice would be this certificate authority (CA) and the delegator denoted by the *Issuer (Alternative) Name*. However, as Casey could create a WebID certificate on his own that contains his WebID URI and Alice's WebID URI, he could also include an adjusted validity period. This would allow him to improperly use Alice's authorization beyond the intended time frame. As a consequence, all delegation constraints specified by the delegator must be also available in her WebID profile.

---

[11] Only Alice, as the primary delegator, can specify the person acting on her behalf.

For the sake of conciseness, not all features of ProProtect3 are discussed here, which we exemplarily implemented in the Sociddea platform. Yet, we offer a public live demonstration of our solution, which is kept up to date and incorporates the latest developments we considered as stable. Further information on page 38.

9   Related Work

This section briefly discusses work related to ours in the context of identity systems in general, and - in particular - mechanisms for access controlling WebID profiles, protecting their integrity and restricting their use in delegation scenarios.

OpenID is an identity system that does not involve a central authority to approve new OpenID identity providers or relying parties [15]. Similar to WebID, it allows identifying users via URIs [12]. OpenID users are enabled to create their own identity provider or choose an existing one [18]. Hackett and Hawkey describe in [18] that OpenID's adoption been initially hindered by *"inconsistencies in the sign-in interface"*, but increased since major IT companies like Google offered own OpenID identity providers. While not limited, OpenID is typically deployed using passwords as proof of a user's identity. Florencio and Herley discuss in [16] that this can cause issues summarized by the term "password fatigue", i.e., a vast number of passwords users need to remember, poor password quality and high password redundancy. WebID users can self-manage their profile data in a flexible, extensible, and machine-readable way, whereas OpenID only offers limited handling of personal attributes [20]. Unlike WebID, OpenID does not rely on client certificates, which makes it compatible with more Web browsers.

Mozilla Persona is a single sign-on system which relies on email addresses as identifiers instead of URIs used in WebID or OpenID [1,2]. To prove ownership of an email address, an identity provider issues a certificate to a trusted user, which expires within 24 hours [3]. WebID certificates do not have such static expiration time. While email providers are primarily intended as certificate issuers, Mozilla acts as a fallback. Both Persona and WebID allow users for deciding whether to share their identity with a service provider [18]. Unlike other identity systems, *"Persona requires JavaScript"*[12] as it performs cryptographic operations directly on the client side. Hackett and Hawkey discovered that Persona is vulnerable to phishing attacks due to malicious manipulation of login Web pages [18].

Windows Cardspace tries to provide a consistent digital identity experience by representing each identity of a user by a so-called InfoCard which is *"analogous to physical membership card"* [18,27]. An InfoCard links to an identity provider storing the sensitive data [24]. Cardspace users require a specialized user agent to select their identity [10]. That is, browser vendors would have to add support for this technology [24]. Cardspace allows both self-asserted and managed InfoCards [27], which are comparable to self-signed and CA-signed X.509

---

[12] https://developer.mozilla.org/en-US/docs/Mozilla/Persona/FAQ.

certificates. A user can assign values to an InfoCard's attributes, but the set of attributes is neither extensible nor machine-readable [27]. Although Microsoft decided to stop all efforts for Cardspace in 2011, there are open-source projects like *Open InfoCard*[13] which adopted the InfoCard concept and evolved it.

The next paragraphs discuss access control mechanisms for WebID profiles.

Web Access Control (WAC) is a vocabulary to define access rights to resources at the document level [23]. Requesting agents and agent classes are supported as entities to define access rights to. ACLs specified by WAC[14] are machine-readable through RDF and can be stored independently from the resources they protect. As described by Chudnovskyy et al. in [8], WAC is well-suited for scenarios involving many resources to control access to. Yet, WAC does not support directly controlling access to specific data within resources, e.g., data within WebID profiles. Outsourcing specific data as self-contained resources enables more control with WAC, but complicates maintenance. This is because the number of resources required for a less coarse-grained control increases with the complexity of the data to control access to. For instance, a fine-grained control at its best would result in outsourcing almost each triple of a WebID profile, which describes diverse person attributes, to a separate resource. When applying changes, this approach is inflexible. Additionally, such data distribution and related definition of corresponding ACLs comes along with declining portability.

Access Control Ontology (ACO) is similar to WAC, but adds support for roles and enables directly mapping permissions to HTTP verbs [36]. To protect data within resources with ACO, relevant data has to be outsourced to separate resources. ACO and WAC share the same maintainability and portability issues.

The *"data perspective"* approach proposed by Tramp et al. customizes WebID profile data for particular profile requesters by introducing sets of triples as alternative information sources [39]. For each combination of requested information, requester and public key, a view is defined in terms of the set of triples to be returned. While WAC and ACO only enable controlling access to resources, this vocabulary allows manipulating data represented by resources. These view definitions increase flexibility by providing improved filter expressiveness, e.g., new triples can be directly added to the profile view. However, profile data is distributed across both the view definitions and the actual WebID profile. This decreases maintainability because updating requires changes in several places. If view definitions are used as an additional layer of information, profile data would be stored in two different places, which bears the risk of creating conflicts. Unlike the approach proposed in this article, it does not support group-wise views.

After describing related access control facilities, the following part discusses techniques for data integrity protection and verification of RDF documents.

The *Public Key Infrastructure* (PKI) is a set of hardware, software, people, policies, and procedures needed to create, manage, store, distribute, and revoke digital certificates [37]. A PKI is used for creating trustworthy certification chains and provides an infrastructure to verify the integrity of signed certificates. The PKI defines so-called Certification Authorities (CA) which issue certificates after

---

[13] https://code.google.com/p/openinfocard/.

[14] http://www.w3.org/ns/auth/acl.

a strong review process, i.e., the owner of a CA-signed certificate has to prove intensely to be the identity claimed. Due to this PKI validation process, a PKI integration into WebID would increase the effort of creating new WebID certificates by users. While a PKI associates certificates with real world identities, a WebID identity should be more anonymous to provide privacy. Additionally, a PKI has several disadvantages discussed by Ellison and Schneier in [13].

To calculate hashes of RDF graphs, Sayers and Karp propose another approach in [32]. While in the ProProtect3 approach RDF graphs are signed in there canonical representation [7], Sayers and Karp expand the RDF graph to assign a unique label to each blank node. These labels are defined as new statements which should not change the semantic of the original RDF graph. To sign the blank nodes within an RDF graph, they are named with these labels. So, the hash value of an RDF graph does not depend on the blank node identifiers.

Finally, related work for delegation in the WebID context is explained next.

A widely adopted protocol for authorization is *OAuth* [19]. It has been designed to allow users to grant third-party services access to their personal resources without disclosing their private credentials. The protocol flow in brief: The *Client* requesting access to a protected resource retrieves an *Authorization Grant* from the *Resource Owner*. It presents this grant to the *Authorization Server*, which validates it, and receives an *Access Token*. Using the token, the *Client* can now request the protected resource from the *Resource Server*. Evidently, this is a delegation of access rights from the *Resource Owner* to the *Client*.

In [39] an extension of the WebID protocol for access delegation is discussed. The approach distinguishes between a *principal* and a *secretary* role. A statement specifying a trusted secretary's WebID in the principal's WebID profile allows the secretary to act on behalf of the principal. The secretary adds an X-On-Behalf-Of header to the HTTP request to get access on the principal's behalf. First, the server checks the provided WebID authenticating the secretary. To check the claimed on-behalf-of relationship to the principal's WebID given in the request header, the server dereferences the principal's WebID profile. If it contains a :secretary statement confirming the claim, the secretary is authorized to access the requested resource with the same access rights as the principal.

Summary. Identity systems like OpenID, Persona etc. do not allow users to maintain full control of their personal data when deployed by third parties. They are limited in attaching and exchanging data to identities, whereas WebID enables users to self-host, self-manage and publish their profile data in an expressive, extensible and machine-readable way using Linked Data. Access control mechanisms typically provide coarse-grained protection of resources. Fine-grained protection often requires outsourcing data to diverse resources or creating additional data layers for specific requesters, which impairs maintainability and portability. Unlike them, ProProtect3 enables fine-grained filters for profile data which are expressive and fit into the way data is stored in WebID profiles. While a PKI based on CAs represents a centralized trust model that would allow for discovering profile data tampering and identity theft, ProProtect3 follows a different path that does not interfere with WebID's decentralized approach of empowering individuals instead of authorities. Similar to the delegation approaches we have discussed, ProProtect3 facilitates separation between delegatee and delegator. Contrary to them, it only reuses the existing (WebID) artifacts and infrastructure components (client, service provider, identity provider). Like OAuth, ProProtect3 enables defining constraints for a delegation, e.g., service or duration of delegation.

10   Conclusions and Future Work

In this article we proposed the ProProtect3 approach that allows identity owners (1) to control the way their semantically-enabled profile data is exposed to others, (2) to verify the data integrity of profiles, and (3) to prevent improper use in delegation scenario by introducing restrictions. We presented and analyzed typical usage, risk, and attack scenarios. They indicated the need for an extensive protection against unwanted retrieval, malicious change, and inappropriate use in the context of knowledge centered systems and Linked Data. By developing both a theoretical foundation and practical implementations for fine-grained profile views, profile protection against forgery, and restriction of rights of persons acting on others' behalves, we substantiated our threefold approach relying on Linked Open Data and, thus, contributed to the Semantic Web vision. We demonstrated ProProtect3 by its exemplary integration into the Sociddea WebID identity provider.

Summary of main contributions. With the introduction of requester-specific filters on WebID profile data, identity owners are enabled to keep control about amount and nature of personal data being presented to entities requesting their profile data. We defined a filter vocabulary for this purpose. This part of ProProtect3 also established a fallback mechanism to automatically select the best-matching filter depending on the requester. To cover almost all scenarios of hiding and showing specifics within profiles, we used SPARQL CONSTRUCT statements as filter commands. We recommend whitelisting non-sensitive profile data per requester and exclude all filter specifications during filtering.

By verifying the data integrity of WebID profiles with ProProtect3, profile requesters can ensure that data stored within was not manipulated. Neither on the server hosting their WebID profiles nor during transmission. When data disclosure would not be an issue, this *theoretically* enables users, who have only a small IT skill set, to host their WebID profile on untrusted or insecure systems. As another significant benefit of this contribution, subjects can easily prove that they are in control of the resource representing their WebID profile. This can be done by comparing the SHA-256 hash value of a public key contained within a WebID certificate with the hash part of an integrity-enabled WebID URI.

With the design of a new delegation procedure considering security as a primary principle, the profile data of delegators is protected through ProProtect3 against improper use by the subjects acting on their behalves. The ProProtect3 delegation approach is backward-compatible and easy to combine with the approaches for protection from tampering and unwanted retrieval. Tampering of user profile data is detected by checking the WebID URI and profile of both delegator and delegatee. Combined with ProProtect3's disclosure protection, it enables customized views on the profile data of an identity owner, who is also the delegator, for the delegatee and for the service to be used. Besides allowing for clearly distinguishing between the delegator and subjects acting on his behalf, a delegator can set constraints to avoid improper use of profile data by delegatees.

Roadmap to future work. Having created a foundation to protect WebID profile data with the ProProtect3 approach, future work will proceed from there to substantiate and extend this approach, as explained in the following.

A comprehensive evaluation would allow for indicating the benefits and deficits of the approach in practice. As a first step, a platform integrating ProProtect3 must reach a critical user mass for enabling sound experimental validation results. By focusing the evaluation on performance and user acceptance, we would be able to determine how much ProProtect3 contributes to the adoption of WebID.

To evolve the fine-grained filtering of user profile data, we will analyze filter cascades. We think applying several filters in specific sequences is beneficial for combining protection needs. We also want to facilitate reusing filters by sharing them between users of a distributed social network. Furthermore, it might be interesting to apply customized views on user profile data which selectively add or modify data. Finally, customized views based on more than one profile would allow creating information sets about groups and keeping them up to date.

For substantiating ProProtect3's protection against malicious change of profile data, we would like to conduct a user study. Our intention behind this user study is to find out how users get along with integrity-enabled WebID URIs. While such WebID URIs are not an issue when processed by machines, they might be problem for human beings. According to our experience, users choose WebID URIs they can remember. They do this even though it is not necessary because an issued WebID certificate includes the WebID URI linking to the associated WebID profile. Besides this, further research is required on the topic of using multiple keys for signature creation and verification. At the moment, an identity owner is limited to use only one particular key pair, i.e., one WebID certificate, for this task. This has disadvantages in terms of flexibility, portability, and operation, which we would like to address by allowing more than one key pair for signing.

Web-based crowdsourcing enables to outsource tasks to a large yet undefined group of individuals via an open call. Here, the potential delegation target is unknown before accepting the task offer. To manage such scenario, the proposed delegation procedure needs to relax the restriction of assigning a task to a particular delegatee. So, we will research the delegation involving groups of known as well as unknown subjects while protecting the delegator's WebID profile data against improper use. We also want to perform a more extensive analysis on the constraints that might be significant for delegators, e.g., more precise service restrictions or budget restrictions for travel bookings. Last but not least, we plan to remove the restriction of only assigning one task per delegatee at the same time by independently handling delegator and task descriptions.

Finally, we will further work towards our vision that WebID profiles are used as descriptions of services and components of a Web system. Using WebID profiles would allow to store service-specific data in a machine-readable way and enable authentication between services of a Web system. As an example, information about a service's connections as well as internal data on utilization, mean time between failures, maintenance costs etc. could be presented to other authorized services. We are of the view that analyzing this data will assist predicting the evolution of Web systems and, consequently, enable to take appropriate measures to guide the Web system's evolution in the right direction as proposed in [44].

Demonstration

Further information to our solution including a link to the Sociddea WebID identity provider and profile management platform is available at: http://vsr.informatik.tu-chemnitz.de/demo/sociddea/.

Acknowledgment. Parts of this work were supported and funded by the European Commission (project OMELETTE, contract 257635).

The authors thank Markus Ast, Falko Braune, Dominik Pretzsch and Michel Rienäcker for their first experimental results on JavaScript-based WebID certificate creation and integrity protection, which have been partially used in this work.

References

1. Akhawe, D., Li, F., He, W., et al.: Data-Confined HTML5 Applications. Technical Report, Electrical Engineering and Computer Sciences, UCB (2013)
2. Bai, G., Lei, J., Meng, G., et al.: AuthScan: Automatic extraction of web authentication protocols from implementations. In: Proceedings of 20th Annual Network & Distributed System Security Symposium (2013)
3. Bamberg, W., et al.: Persona - Protocol Overview (2013). https://developer. mozilla.org/en-US/docs/Mozilla/Persona/Protocol_Overview. Accessed 24 March 2014
4. Barker, E., Barker, W., Burr, W., et al.: NIST Special Publication 800–57: Recommendation for Key Management - Part 1: General (Revision 3). Technical Report, National Institute of Standards and Technology (2012)
5. Bonneau, J., Anderson, J., Anderson, R., Stajano, F.: Eight friends are enough: Social graph approximation via public listings. In: Proceedings of the 2nd ACM EuroSys Workshop on Social Network Systems, pp. 13–18 (2009)
6. Brickley, D., Miller, L.: FOAF Vocabulary Specification 0.99 (2014). http://xmlns. com/foaf/spec/. Accessed 24 March 2014

7. Carroll, J.J.: Signing RDF graphs. In: Fensel, D., Sycara, K., Mylopoulos, J. (eds.) ISWC 2003. LNCS, vol. 2870, pp. 369–384. Springer, Heidelberg (2003)
8. Chudnovskyy, O., Wild, S., Gebhardt, H., Gaedke, M.: Data portability using Webcomposition/Data grid service. Int. J. Adv. Internet Technol. **4**(3 and 4), 123–132 (2012)
9. Cooper, D.: Internet X.509 Public key infrastructure certificate and certificate revocation list (CRL) profile (2008). http://tools.ietf.org/html/rfc5280. Accessed 10 August 2013
10. Dhamija, R., Dusseault, L.: The seven flaws of identity management: Usability and security challenges. IEEE Secur. Priv. **6**(2), 24–29 (2008)
11. Dierks, T.: The Transport Layer Security (TLS) Protocol Version 1.2 (2008). http://tools.ietf.org/html/rfc5246. Accessed 10 August 2013
12. El Maliki, T., Seigneur, J.M.: A survey of user-centric identity management technologies. In: International Conference on Emerging Security Information, Systems, and Technologies. SecureWare 2007, pp. 12–17. IEEE (2007)
13. Ellison, C., Schneier, B.: Ten risks of PKI: What you're not being told about public key infrastructure. Comput. Secur. **16**(1), 1–7 (2000)
14. European Commission: ICT - Work Programme 2013. EC (2012)
15. Fitzpatrick, B., Recordon, D., Hardt, D., Hoyt, J.: OpenID Authentication 2.0 - Final (2007). http://openid.net/specs/openid-authentication-2_0.html. Accessed 10 August 2013
16. Florencio, D., Herley, C.: A large-scale study of web password habits. In: Proceedings of the 16th International Conference on World Wide Web, pp. 657–666. ACM Press (2007)
17. Gellman, B., Poitras, L.: U.S., British Intelligence Mining Data from Nine U.S. Internet Companies in Broad Secret Program. The Washington Post, 6 June 2013
18. Hackett, M., Hawkey, K.: Security, privacy and usability requirements for federated identity. In: Workshop on Web 2.0 Security & Privacy (2012)
19. Hardt, D.: The OAuth 2.0 Authorization Framework (2012). http://tools.ietf.org/html/rfc6749. Accessed 24 March 2014
20. Hardt, D., Bufu, J., Hoyt, J.: OpenID Attribute Exchange 1.0 - Final (2007). http://openid.net/specs/openid-attribute-exchange-1_0.html. Accessed 24 March 2014
21. Harris, S., Seaborne, A.: SPARQL 1.1 Query Language (2013). http://www.w3.org/TR/sparql11-query/. Accessed 24 March 2014
22. Heitmann, B., Kim, J.G., Passant, A., et al.: An architecture for privacy-enabled user profile portability on the Web of Data. In: Proceedings of the 1st International Workshop on Information Heterogeneity and Fusion in Recommender Systems, HetRec 2010, pp. 16–23. ACM (2010)
23. Hollenbach, J., et al.: Using RDF metadata to enable access control on the social semantic web. In: Proceedings of the Workshop on Collaborative Construction, Management and Linking of Structured Knowledge (2009)
24. Jøsang, A., Zomai, M.A., Suriadi, S.: Usability and privacy in identity management architectures. In: Proceedings of the Fifth Australasian Symposium on ACSW Frontiers, vol. **68**, pp. 143–152. Australian Computer Society (2007)
25. Josefsson, S.: The Base16, Base32, and Base64 Data Encodings (2006). http://tools.ietf.org/html/rfc4648. Accessed 24 March 2014

26. Kasten, A., Scherp, A.: Iterative signing of RDF(S) graphs, named graphs, and OWL graphs: Formalization and application. Arbeitsberichte aus dem Fachbereich Informatik **3**, 3–28 (2013)
27. Maler, E., Reed, D.: The venn of identity: Options and issues in federated identity management. IEEE Secur. Priv. **6**(2), 16–23 (2008)
28. Manola, F., Miller, E.: RDF Primer (2004). http://www.w3.org/TR/rdf-primer/. Accessed 29 January 2014
29. Pérez, J., Arenas, M., Gutierrez, C.: Semantics and complexity of SPARQL. ACM Trans. Database Syst. **34**(3), 1–45 (2009)
30. Rivest, R.L., et al.: A method for obtaining digital signatures and public-key cryptosystems. Commun. ACM **21**(2), 120–126 (1978)
31. Savitz, E., Medrano, R.: Welcome To The API Economy - Forbes (2012). http://www.forbes.com/sites/ciocentral/2012/08/29/welcome-to-the-api-economy/. Accessed 24 March 2014
32. Sayers, C., Karp, A.H.: Computing the Digest of an RDF Graph. Mobile and Media Systems Laboratory, HP Laboratories, Palo Alto (2004)
33. Seaborne, A.: SPARQL 1.1 Property Paths (2010). http://www.w3.org/TR/sparql11-property-paths/. Accessed 24 March 2014
34. Sporny, M., Inkster, T., Story, H., et al.: WebID 1.0: Web Identification and Discovery (2011). http://www.w3.org/2005/Incubator/webid/spec/. Accessed 10 Feb 2014
35. The Nielsen Company: Social Media Report 2012 (2012). http://blog.nielsen.com/nielsenwire/social/2012/. Accessed 9 March 2014
36. Tomaszuk, D., Gaedke, M., Gebhardt, H.: WebID+ACO: A distributed identification mechanism for social web. In: Proceedings of the Federated Social Web Europe (2011)
37. Toorani, M., Beheshti, A.: LPKI-a lightweight public key infrastructure for the mobile environments. In: 11th IEEE Singapore International Conference on Communication Systems, 2008, ICCS 2008, pp. 162–166. IEEE (2008)
38. Tramp, S., Frischmuth, P., Ermilov, T., Shekarpour, S., Auer, S.: An architecture of a distributed semantic social network. Semant. Web **5**(1), 77–95 (2012)
39. Tramp, S., Story, H., Sambra, A., et al.: Extending the WebID protocol with access delegation. In: Proceedings of the Third International Workshop on Consuming Linked Data (COLD2012) (2012)
40. Tummarello, G., Morbidoni, C., Puliti, P., Piazza, F.: Signing individual fragments of an RDF graph. In: Special Interest Tracks and Posters of the 14th International Conference on WWW, pp. 1020–1021. ACM (2005)
41. Wild, S., Ast, M., Gaedke, M.: Towards a context-aware WebID certificate creation taking individual conditions and trust needs into account. In: Proceedings of the 15th International Conference on Information Integration and Web-based Applications & Services, pp. 532–541. ACM (2013a)
42. Wild, S., Chudnovskyy, O., Heil, S., Gaedke, M.: Customized views on profiles in webid-based distributed social networks. In: Daniel, F., Dolog, P., Li, Q. (eds.) ICWE 2013. LNCS, vol. 7977, pp. 498–501. Springer, Heidelberg (2013)
43. Wild, S., Chudnovskyy, O., Heil, S., Gaedke, M.: Protecting user profile data in WebID-based social networks through fine-grained filtering. In: Sheng, Q.Z., Kjeldskov, J. (eds.) ICWE Workshops 2013. LNCS, vol. 8295, pp. 269–280. Springer, Heidelberg (2013)

44. Wild, S., Gaedke, M.: WebComposition/EMS: A value-driven approach to evolution. In: Rossi, G., Iturrioz, J. (eds.) ICWE 2009 Doctoral Consortium, pp. 39–43. Onekin Research Group (2009)
45. Yeung, C.M.A., Liccardi, I., Lu, K., et al.: Decentralization: The future of online social networking. In: W3C Workshop on the Future of Social Networking Position Papers, vol. 2, pp. 2–7 (2009)

Author Index

Printed in the United States
By Bookmasters